Sex, drugs and signing the dole

Sex, drugs and signing the dole

Growing up in a Glasgow pub

Joe Reavey

To my dad and drinking buddy
Arthur Reavey thanks for the education..

To Tricia, Shawnay, and Lucas, you are
the moon and stars in my dark life..

Contents

I WISH I KNEW
THEN
WHAT I KNOW
NOW.

CHAPTER 1

Compost Corner

Right, where do we start? No point in starting at the beginning because I'm no' famous so who's going to give a fuck how my childhood was, growing up? No let's start at about 15 years old, just when I went for my first pint of beer. Yeah! That's right - I said 15. Well after all, it is a Glasgow story. Yeah! so I'm 15 years old. My mum and dad split up when I was 7 because the old man loved beer and Elvis more than his family, so I didn't see much of him from 7 to 15. He was busy in the pub. We lived in Pollok which was a real shithole; good people but the tenements were damp and rundown. My mum got an offer from the housing to move to Penilee which she jumped at. I wasn't for going; you know how it is when you're 15. You don't know any better. All I knew was I was going to miss my pals, but I knew it was going to happen anyway. My mum was wanting to be beside her family who all lived in Penilee.

We moved from staying in a wee, damp flat to a back and front door. We became snobs in one flit. I went from sharing a room with my two big brothers to having two rooms to myself. Before you think how big was the house, it had 3 bedrooms. The funny thing is that after 15 years of sharing with my 2 brothers, getting on each other's nerves and trying to kill each other, as soon as we got a bigger house they moved out - bye. Arthur went into the RAF and Gerry, the army. Both of them went to get out of Glasgow and find work and a better life, which they both did I'm happy to say. So, I'm feeling like I'm in a new chapter in my life but I was feeling lost back then.

I knew school was coming to an end and I was fine with that as I didn't get anything out of it. I knew it was a lost cause for me. I don't want to make out that school is pointless or anything - far from it. I was just a daft kid who didn't know how to spell, so always found it hard trying to study, and when you can't spell all you want to do is get out of school so you don't have to. And I was in the fourth year, getting into trouble just to get them to kick me out, as I knew my time with school was up. So I was looking forward to getting out into the big, bad world and making some money with my hands because my head wasn't going to make much, was it?

Right let's get back to being lost. It was 1990 and the start of the nineties was shit. Some films were OK but the music was so bad. I didn't know much about good bands like the Stones or the Beatles till I met my mates in Penilee. The nineties music was only saved when Oasis showed up, thank fuck. Then there was football which I'm no' into that much, but in Glasgow football is life. You are a Celtic fan or a Rangers fan and you get on with your life fighting over who's the best team and who's the shit team, easy. So, for a young kid like me no' being into football I was the odd kid out. Well no' just me. My brother, Arthur, didn't like it either, and I'm sure that must have killed my dad inside. I mean, the shame of it! Your kids no' liking the game. What will the guys at work think if they find out? I'm sure my dad was thinking they must be big fucking Jessies if they don't like the Celtic. My brother, Gerry, was. and still is, a die-hard Celtic fan so as Meatloaf sang, 'two out of three ain't bad'. Being a young kid in Pollok in the eighties was tough but we didn't know any better. All the kids in the street were in the same boat – all skint - so having a football would keep you busy, but no' liking football left you with fuck all to do. I mean, if it wasn't for my dick I would have had nothing to play with.

My mum got a job in Haddows, the off-sale shop, when we moved to Penilee which was good news for me as she worked 9 till 11.30 Monday to Friday, which meant I didn't need to be in a hurry to go to school at 9am; I could have a lie in as long as I was out the house for 11, to let the fire go cold before she got home. One Monday morning, well, almost afternoon, I was walking to school on the Paisley Road West, just passing the Cardonald Library when this guy stops me and says, "Joseph son, how you doing?" I'm like, yeah, I'm good, at the same time as I'm thinking, "who the fuck is this?" The sun was in my eyes and then it hits me, it's my dad. Out of the past seven years I'd only seen him about a handful of times, the last time being maybe two years ago. He was happy to see me and I was, too. He asked me to pop down and see my granny when I could because, "she keeps asking for you and your brothers," so I'm thinking, yeah, I can pop down this week, maybe and get a day off school.

I say to him, "I'll come down and see her this Friday, about 11",

and he looks with a smile on his face and says, "don't you

have school to go to on a Friday?"

He gives me a hug and says, "OK son, see you Friday, and I'll tell your gran you're coming to cheer her up". As I'm about to walk away he says, "maybe after you see your gran we could go to the pub for a Coke?"

I walked away thinking, how cool would that be? All my pals will be in school and I'll be in the pub. I remember those four days dragging by longer then a two week self-catering holiday in Iraq, so on Friday I decided to show up and I had that weekend feeling. I went to see my wee granny and she made a fuss over me like a gran does trying to feed me, and giving me a few bucks and then saying what she always said, "don't tell your dad I gave you money". My dad sat doing his crossword like he did every day just to kill time before going to the pub and my ass was making buttons wanting to go, but he was in no hurry. To him it was the same pub, day in day out, so it hits about 2 o'clock and we were off to the pub for a Coke.

I don't know if everyone remembers their first time going for a pint but I remember that day like it was yesterday. My dad opened the door for me and I walked in feeling like Dorothy walking into the Land of Oz. I was so nervous but was trying to keep my cool. The floor tiles and the brass bars round the bar where shining; it was spotless to me but to be fair it had only been opening time about two hours before so no one had been sick yet or walked in with their work boots on needing a hangover cure. Old Maureen, the barmaid, asked my dad, "what you having?" He says, "give me a pint of tartan special," and then he looks at me and says, "do you want a Coke or do you want a pint?" I said the word 'pint' faster than the speed of sound. Then he hits out with, "do you want a pint of beer or a pint of lager?" Now asking a 15 year-old kid if he wants beer or lager makes no sense, because all I was thinking is, whatever - they both get me drunk. It's like asking me if I want to spend the night with Pamela Anderson or Pamela Fae Anderson. Anyway I went for beer, a fine choice I'm thinking. Old Maureen puts it down beside me and says to my dad, "is he no' too young?" to which my dad tells her to shut it. I'm thinking inside, yeah, fuck up Maureen.

I took that cold pint with both hands like it was the holy grail, lifted it like it was the fucking world cup and took my first sip of a pint; no' my first sip of beer - that was way back when I was about 5 years-old. You know when your dad would go for a piss and you and your brothers would down his can before he got back. No, this was my first pint, my first jar with the boys – well, my dad and a few old guys sitting filling in their bookie slips. We stood at the end of the bar and my dad knew everyone. They all said hi as they passed. It was like Cheers; I couldn't take it all in. I was so busy enjoying every sip of my beer till my dad says, "go easy on that. I'm no' made of money !" I was standing looking round the pub thinking this is it, what I've been looking for my whole young life - something to be good at and I was sure I would be good at drinking beer.

So, I have my pint of beer in hand and I'm trying to play it cool like it's just another day at the boozer. My dad says, "let's get a seat". We head over to the corner of the pub, the corner that would become known as Compost Corner. It got

its name a few years later because of my dad's best mate, Big
Rab Fraser (who we'll get to at some point in the story, just
no' yet because just now in this bit he is doing time). So, Big
Rab Fraser walked in one Friday night after his work, went to
the bar to get a beer, looked over at the corner to see who was
in and saw about ten or more of us all drinking and smoking
dope, and said, "fuck me, it's like Compost Corner over there,"
and from that night it stuck.

That first day in the Argosy bar the first guy I met was
Mick Boyle and he asked me, "are you still at school or have
you left ?" I said I'd left school because really, I had; like I said,
I was done with school and he said right, now your education
for the real world begins today, and God, he was so spot on.
My dad and Mick had theses long running jokes, like old Chic
Murray jokes; he would say, "how's the divorce going, Mick
and Mick would say, "all good, Arthur, me and the wife split
the house fifty-fifty. She got the inside and I got the outside."
Or my dad would say, "I went to a whore house, Mick, and
a young good-looking girl asked me if I would like super sex,
and I said I'll have the soup, thanks". It didn't matter how
many times some of the guys told the same jokes, they never
got old, and if someone asked my dad how he was he would
always say, "wonderful darling, just wonderful," even if he was
sitting there skint waiting for someone to buy him his next
beer. One of the best jokes I was told was the guy who went
to the doctors' thinking he was dying. The doctor asked him,
"what's wrong?" The guy says, "my whole body hurts. I'm in
so much pain". The doctor asked again, "where does it hurt?"
The guy says, "everywhere I touch. If I touch my chest it's

painful, or my head or even my leg. Everywhere I touch I'm in pain". The doctor takes a look and examines him and says, "you daft cunt, you've broken your finger".

The guys in the pub were all in the same boat so they didn't tell everyone about their troubles. They were all going through the same shit in life, like alcohol and drug addiction, or being married and your wife is a cunt, or no' being married because your wife is a cunt, they all had the same story to tell so the best thing to do was don't tell it, just get on with it and get drunk. That first day in the Argosy bar was like a school trip for me. My dad introduced me to all of his pals; most of them someday I would call my pals, too. As we were sitting having that beer Big John and Rab D came in and my dad says, "do you like hash?" And I'm like, "sure" and then he says, "let's go to the bogs for a smoke, then, with Big John". As we were standing in the toilets all the boys showed up, all talking away to my dad and me and I'm thinking, this is way better than sitting in school. We went back to our seats, got another beer and I remember just sitting there knowing this is going to be my local, my second home, just like my dad and my grandad, Joe Reavey, before him. All the guys and their families - that made the pub what it was, because a pub is only as good as the people who drink in it, and the Argosy bar had some gang!

My dad said to me that day, "I remember being your age, standing outside this pub looking in at your grandad and wishing I was in there having a beer, and now I'm sitting here with you, son. Time goes too fast". He was right because in the blink of an eye I now sit and have a beer with my kid in

15

the Argosy bar. I sit and look around and think about times gone by: all the good times and bad times, all the mad, funny and crazy guys and girls over the years that popped in for a drink. If the walls of the pub could talk, well, I wouldn't need to write this book. I just hope I can put these stories down on paper - all the funny and sad times in the Argosy Bar and how you find out the hard way that time waits for no one.

The things most guys like about a pub is somewhere to go and talk to the boys about anything, the place to go on your day off work - well, after you get the family stuff out the way (like spending time with the kids and talking to the wife for more than 5 minutes). My dad once told me that when me and my brothers were small my mum would suggest that they should take us kids to the park and my dad would always talk his way out of it so he could get to the pub for a beer and see his pals.

He said, "back when my boys were wee, I thought they would be young kids forever, so there was always time to take the kids to the park next week. And before you know it you're an old man and your boys are all grown up." He said that the biggest mistake a young guy makes in his life is thinking he is going to be young forever. "I would see guys popping in for a quick beer on their way home from work - that one I never got! I mean, why would you want to have just one beer. Never made any sense to me, but then again, I was always a young greedy fucker."

I would ask my dad, "why do you think some guys pop in for just one beer?"

He said, "maybe they were no' in a hurry to get home

because their wives were cunts".

And I was like, "OK, maybe, or perhaps they're alcoholics who were hiding it from the wife because if she found out they would be out of the big bed".

I would sit as a young kid and think how sad it was that some guys' lives are just a lie, putting up with shit and sneaking about in a pub just to keep the peace with the wife. Most of the guys in the Argosy Bar weren't in for a jolly up on their day off, or in for just the one pint. No. Most of them were in the pub because the good lady in their lives told them to get their ass down the road a bit, and don't come back. These guys were in the pub killing time. The eighties were over and the nineties didn't look any better in the way of jobs. Most guys in Glasgow and all over the UK had lost their jobs and with no work, and too much time on their hands, what were they going to do? You drink because drink is a great way to kill time and before you know it you've lost a lot more than just your job. It must have been a hard time back then, all these guys lost with no jobs, all the days of working in the ship yards for years, then nothing but the dole. And when you go to sign on they say you can go and work in Safeway as a shelf stacker, and there's nothing wrong with that, but it's a big drop from being a ship builder.

In the Argosy every now and then an old face would show up: some guy standing at the bar looking like a spare prick at a wedding. My dad and his pals would try and work out where they knew him from and it would turn out he was an old school or work mate and he, like many others, had been told by his wife to do one. They all looked the same standing holding a beer, looking like lost souls. These guys were known as 'my baby left me' and everyone knew to stay away from them, to leave them be, because they were looking to bust someone's, anyone's, ears about how they had fallen on hard times, how the wife was coming in from the bingo all red-faced and sweating. If you saw someone talking to a stranger at the bar and you said, "who's that Rab is talking to?" someone would say, "I worked with that guy," and you would say, "yeah, what's his story," and they would hit out with "my baby left me" and that said it all. You knew to keep out of his way or you were going to get bored to death. A pub is always going to have a few lost souls in it because when your life is going down the bog, where else better is there than a pub to drink some girl off your mind? There's nothing better than sitting with the boys talking shit over a few cold beers and maybe a joint, or a few lines, whatever gets you through the night. You know there are people who pay a lot of money to sit with a psychiatrist and tell them their troubles in life. Fuck that! Go to the pub and tell it there. All it will cost you is the price of a few beers and there's always someone willing to listen to you as long as you're buying; and the good thing is they have probably been through what you're going through, and will give you better advice than some rich, happily married psychologist whose life is different from yours, so what would they know?

Now the unwritten rule with smoking dope in the pub was, as when I first went into the Argosy, you had to go to the toilet to smoke the joints and everyone would wait 5 minutes then come in, but you couldn't all get up and walk in at the same time single file, that would look bad, so you had to go in one at a time. It was like being in the war, going over the top one at a time, 'see you on the other side old chap, and tell little Tommy I won't be coming home this Christmas', but the funny thing was the barmaids knew exactly what we were up to. Now the thing that did look really bad was when some poor guy who didn't know us was in there having a piss, and he sees two guys going into the same cubicle and hears shit like "pull it out" and "lick them, yeah, now burn it up" and the best one – "do you want a blow back?" Smoking in the bogs was mad. Everyone would go in the one cubicle - about six guys - and shut the door, blocked the air vent so that the smoke would stay in the cubicle, and you were told once you're in you don't get out. I found this out after I had gone in one day and I was, like, "right, I don't feel too good," and I was told, "don't worry only four joints to go till we're done". So even if you had a few draws and then you started to feel it was too much and you stopped smoking, you were still taking it in; it would hit you like a ton of bricks and I would be trying to keep up, feeling that I had to prove myself to the boys. My dad and his pal, Stevie, were in the toilet rolling one day when Stevie dropped his wee bit of hash. He bent down to pick it up, got it, and to make sure it was hash he took a bite at it to find out the hard way it was a wee bit of shit - some old drunk guy's shit - no' that it makes it any better or worse, I mean shit is shit.

The good thing was that after about a year we didn't need to hide in the toilet. We could smoke in the corner just as long as we didn't roll up at the table as that would be asking for trouble if the cops walked in. So we would still roll in the bogs, but no more whitey for me hugging the pan, trying to work out how I'm going to get home.

Going back to my first day, the second guy I met was Big John Bonnie. John was a great guy; he should have been a stand-up comedian - you would be pissing yourself at his shit jokes and one liners. He would always have a suit on and a bit of gold on his fingers. He was the Del-boy of the Argosy, well, one of a few who looked like he had money, but he got by from week to week working at the races with his old man, doing tick tack. I was in the pub one day when John came in.

I asked him, "how's things, mate?"

John.. "Bad son. Some dirty cunt broke into my house last night."

Me.. "You're kidding! Did they take much?"

John.. "Yeah they took my mum's gold rings and our video player."

Me.. "Dirty fuckers."

John.. "But you know, what really got me mad was my mum had a big pot of mince on the cooker and the dirty fuckers done a shit in it."

me.." No way!"

John.. "Yeah. We had to throw half of it out...

That was John he always had a joke or would do daft stuff like turn a chair upside down and kid on that he was playing the bagpipes. I knew John and drank with him for about 5 years, which seems a long time when you're young. I met him again 10 years later when I was 30. We were at a party and he told me he didn't drink anymore. I asked him why not, and he says, "all my pals are dead and it's because of the drink and I don't want to drink alone". I didn't know what to say to him so I just made a joke and said, "last one out of the taxi pays the price, John". I was so young and didn't have a clue about life back then. At the beginning all I knew was that these guys were having a ball drinking and smoking, and I wanted in on the action so bad. But what I didn't see and what you don't know when you're 15 is that there's a down side to all this. Drink might give you a hangover but in time it will get a hold of you, grab you like a hungry wolf in the night. All the booze and drugs in the world won't work forever and by the time you want to stop the world and get off it's too late. That's the bit the guys in the pub don't show you. No! You'll find that bit out for yourself and like everyone else you'll find out the hard way. One minute you're drinking for fun, then the next you're drinking to keep the wolf from the door.

So there I was thinking I'm all grown up drinking in the pub like a big boy, trying to keep up with my dad and his pals, and constantly being told by my dad to take a back seat and just listen and take it all in, but in the real world outside the pub I was still just a daft wee boy of 15, not knowing if it was New York or New Year. But the first thing I had to do was get a job because I was needing beer tokens if I was wanting to drink in the pub. Trying to get a job in the early nineties was a nightmare. Everyone was out of work so all a young guy could get was a factory job at £1 an hour for 40 hours a week - pure slavery. On I Friday I took home my £40 and gave my mum £20, then I had £20 to spend over the weekend on beer and hash, or maybe stay in one weekend and buy a new top for next weekend. That's just how it was. It was shit but we didn't know any better, and at that young age it was hard to try and impress any girls with only a few bucks in your pocket. I mean, what chance did you have when a girl wants a boyfriend with a car and I didn't even have a fucking bus pass. The best I could offer was a bag of chips and a bottle of 20/20 to wash it down with.

Getting to know females seemed hard work to me. I didn't know what to say and would always try too hard to impress them. When you're young you don't think to yourself 'just be yourself and let them get to know you and if they like you, then happy days'. I remember the first girl who liked me, or took pity on me should I say, she became my first girlfriend. We walked the streets every night, summer or winter, holding hands, then at the end of the night before she had to go home we would hide away in the flats for a wee kiss, and it went on like that for a long time. No touching, just kissing. You could have broken toffee with my dick, it was that hard, but she wasn't up for anything and I was OK with it because she was 15 and I knew the score, but in the pub my dad's pals would give me a hard time about it, going on like, "hey you shagged your wee bird yet?" and if I told them "no" or "yes" I would still get a hard time about it so I didn't say anything. Finally one cold winter's night my wee bird told me, "tonight you can see and have a feel of my boobs". I couldn't walk her fast enough to the flats. I was like Usain Bolt. She lifted her kappa T-shirt and showed me the goods. I went in for a feel, then a kiss, and she didn't seem to mind so I went for it and licked them, like I was licking an ice cream on a hot day. I was in heaven.

On the walk home she made me swear on my life no' to tell anyone because she didn't want a bad name. And as I was telling her I wouldn't talk about her like that my mouth was drying up, and then my throat went really dry and she was still going on about when a girl gets a name for herself it sticks with her forever, like the girl in her class at school; her nickname was chips and beans because she goes with anything. As I burst out laughing I struggled to breathe, my throat was so dry, and then I got the fear - maybe I was allergic to tits. Fucking hell! One lick and a suck and I'm on my way out. But I wasn't. Turned out my wee bird forgot to tell me that she had about half a can of impulse sprayed on, and that I had lick it all off. My mouth was dryer than a nun's cunt. After that getting to know females seemed a walk in the park; just need a wee bit of patter and listen when they talk, and stay away from girls your own age - they all want older boys with cars and money. So I went for older girls like bored housewives.

When I was about 17 a girl in my work on a night out told me, "you have what I need and I have what you need," and I didn't know what she was on about. Then one day in work this older woman - well, when I say old I mean she was about 30, so when you're 17 that's old – anyway, I asked her what she meant at the night out, and she smiled and said, "come to mine this Friday for dinner and I'll tell you". And me being young and dumb says, "will your husband be OK with me coming for dinner?" and she laughed and rubbed my face and says, "my husband works away on the rigs". I went for a pint that day and told the boys. They all went quiet. Then Gerry says, "jammy fucker". Then they made me swear to come to the pub on the Saturday and tell them all about it, which I did, and I was carried shoulder high from the pub. Well no, really my dad did shout, "there's the saint in lads".

I wish I could tell you that Saturday night I spent with the older and very friendly women happened a lot in my teenage years but it didn't. Like most young guys I couldn't get a bird in a pet shop. That's why when most guys get a bird they hold on to them the best they can, even if they're a pain in the ass. Remember all the people from your past and you sit and think, 'why did I put up with that fucker?' Well, I don't know why girls put up with us guys, but I know why we did, because we were on a mission; more like mission impossible for me though. Funny how we spend 9 months trying to get out and the rest of our life trying to get right back in. Any job I had was where I would meet a girl. I never had much luck going into town for a night out. In fact I hated it; paying to get into some shithole club, buying beer at a pound more than it was in the pub, and it was always mobbed and loud so that when you did get to the bar you had to buy two pints because it was that busy. So every guy would be standing hold two beers, trying to look cool. They say that in the nineties ninety five per cent of the women went out only to have a dance and a drink. Yeah, I know. I'm sure I went on a date with every one of them, standing on a sticky dance floor, shouting in some girls ear, making her go deaf in one ear. I found the best night was a works night out because you knew who you had a chance with, so it cut out all the getting to know you shit, and you could hold off till the end of the night to talk to them. That way you didn't need to buy them a drink all night - see, always thinking. The only thing that could go wrong on a works night out is you could get a knock back, then you had to face them on Monday morning; you know, walking into work making out you can't remember. Always blame the drink.

I remember a factory I was working in and a girl in the office was so good looking, but no matter how much I would talk to her she never seemed interested so after a few weeks I gave up. Then one Christmas night out I was half pissed, heading to the toilet and she was on her way back and she was looking really happy to see me, so I'm thinking someone's drunk. She was like, "big Joe, Merry Christmas" and she starts hugging me, and I'm like, yeah, how you doing in the middle of the hugging and her being OK with my hands everywhere. Someone walked past and we stopped and I went for a piss. When I got back to my table she was gone - fucked off like Cinderella. I asked her pal where she went and she said she'd had too much to drink and went home. On the Monday morning at work I went into the office to say hello and see if we were OK but she wasn't in. She'd phoned in sick and stayed on the old 'pat and mick' for weeks. The shame of having a wee roll about with me outside the bogs must have been too much for her. I kept thinking what her sick note might have said - touched up by Joe at the works night out. The boss Mr. Alan like - "we've all been there, take as long as you need, hen". I remember another girl coming back from the sick and someone asking her whether she was OK. She said, "I'm only back with help from the doctor," and I said, "is he giving you a lift to work?"

The other problem was if you were lucky enough for a girl to say yes to a date, where did you take them? I'm ashamed to say I did take girls to the Argosy. I walked in one night thinking to play it cool, wee bird on my arm. Everyone was saying hello to me. Then I asked the girl what she was drinking. "Long vodka please," and the barmaid said, "we don't do cocktails in here, hen," so she got half a cider. It was a nightmare!

Old John asked her if she knew the secret to a good marriage.

"No ,"she said, "what is it?"

and he said, "its only two words... yes dear..".

Just when I was thinking everything was going good, a big guy, Eddie, asked me if we were going to the dancing later.

I said "no, I'm no' into the dancing, Eddie,"

and he said to the girl, "I love the dancing, hen. I just go in, get a pint and look for biggest, ugly girl in the club and go over to her and say drink up, hen, we're out of here".

The girl asked, "does it work?"

"Yeah, most of the time it does".

And me sitting there thinking no it doesn't, Eddie, that's why you're sitting in here on your own. So after that the Argosy was a no go for dates. I stuck to Chinese restaurants and The Pines. The only girl who I've sat drinking in the Argosy with and had a good night is my wife but I knew she would be fine because she is from Govan; she can handle all the mean old fuckers and give as good as she gets.

Sex, drugs and signing the dole

IF YOU FLY WITH
THE CROWS,
YOU GET SHOT
WITH THE
CROWS.

CHAPTER 2

Argosy Gang.

There were five main families in the pub who were called Reavey... Arthur my dad was like most guys in the late eighties and early nineties, out of work and walking round like a lost soul. All these guys who were ship builders, now out of work, trying to find a way to kill time which is hard to do when you're skint. My dad was a proud man, which made it hard being out of work. He spent his days in a routine like he was doing time in jail. He spent his time keeping himself busy so he didn't go mad. He drank in the pub six days a week, but he would only have a about five pints a day, maybe more if someone was buying, but if not it would be five beers, then home. When you're on the dole you have to make what money you have last two weeks. The majority of the guys in the pub were in the same boat, all killing time, but my old man never showed any weakness, he always joked about it; like most Glasgow guys, just cry in your beer and get on with it.

My dad's brother Joe was the local postman. You know when people say he was the nicest guy you could ever meet, well my Uncle Joe was that guy. No one had a bad word to say about him. He lived a quiet life, went to his work, then went home to his wee flat, watched TV and had a wee whisky and a joint or two. He would only go to the pub on a Sunday for a half and a catch up with all the boys. I loved Joe. He was so funny. He would always say stuff like, "my back is killing me, son, I'm stiffer than a honeymooner's prick," and when he would be out on his job, if he found a sweet on the street that someone had spat out he would pick it up and put it in another sweet wrapper and keep it for a Sunday and give it to whatever moody barmaid was on. It was class! I would go, "hi Joe," and he would say "hi" back and I would ask, "you got a wee sweet for the barmaid?" And he would pat his pocket and say, "oh yes,". He would go to the bar with my old man, get a round in then say, "here you go dear, a wee sweetie for you". She would unwrap it and stick it in her mouth and say to my dad, "why can't you be as nice as your brother?" Fucking hell! If she had only known it was covered in dog piss she would have gone nuts. And when he handed it over there were about ten of us waiting to see if the taste was too much, but he got away with it every time.

Joe lived alone. His wife, my Aunty Rena, passed away when I was about six years old. He had three daughters and my dad, three sons. Every Saturday me and my old man would go to Joe's for a drink and a smoke and watch either Elvis, the Beatles or 'Dances with Wolves'. One day I went in and Joe was offering me a whisky and I'm like, "no thanks," because they would never have enough Coca Cola for it, and no ice, but Joe went on and on to take a drink. So he went out of the room. My dad pours me a glass of whisky and a wee drop of coke, and it gets a head on it like a pint of beer and I'm thinking, that's not right, but fuck it, and just as I'm drinking it, Joe comes into the room with a glass for me, to which my dad says, "he won't need that, I gave him the glass I had my Askit powder in" (now only people in Scotland or maybe only Glasgow know about Askit powders) - they were the best pain killer you could find; they were so strong that if you took one with a beer, which I did all the time, your hangover was gone. And they were easy to get. You could buy them off the ice cream van. But they were killing people because of how addictive they were. Now anyone who knows me knows I loved them just like my dad, but no' in my whisky and coke. It looked like a pint of Guinness had been left out all night and I knew I had to drink it because something in your drink was no big deal. The alcohol will take care of it. I remember once sitting in my dad's flat and a spider fell from the ceiling into Joe's whisky glass and as he picked it up, I said, "Joe, stop - a spider fell in your glass". He just downed the lot and then said, "did it, well fuck it, it's the last of the whisky anyway". And another time I spilled my whisky and my dad sucked it up from the fucking carpet. I'm like, fuck sake, we have a full bottle here, get a grip.

We don't need to worry about Askit powders any more. They got token off the shelves in 2006. Askit was the second best drug to take for a hangover, the first being Valium. All the guys were taking them for the fear of when the hangover hits your nerves. My dad says Valium makes you think you're Muhammad Ali, and he was right. I mean, you could be running away from crisp packets walking to the pub for a pint, but take a Valium and you would tap dance into the pub like Gene Kelly.

Law... Gerry law was my dad's big pal. Gerry and my dad sat in the corner six days a week for years. Gerry was one of the money lenders or loan sharks in the pub. He was off the drink when I first met him. When he went on it every now and then, he was the life and soul of the place. He would get so drunk he would sing and tell jokes and play the jukebox all night. He would drink like there was no tomorrow. As a 15 year old kid I looked up to Gerry; he seemed to have the perfect life, making money in the pub, and he always wore a suit with a smart T shirt. I would think, that's a cool job; he's his own boss, shows up when he wants, gets stoned and drunk, and still makes money. But over the years I realized it wasn't a fun job. He sat in the pub bored day in, day out, listening to guys with drink and gambling habits tell him bullshit reasons why they couldn't pay him this week. I asked him one day, "why do you go on and off the drink?" and he says, "I hate the taste of drink but I love being drunk". He got hangovers from hell, too.

Gerry loved to get stoned. He loved it more than the drink. He would have a hot bath every morning so he could smoke a joint in it to get stoned before he went to the pub, and he and my dad were the only guys in the pub who would roll their joints before they left home. It made perfect sense; the rest of us had to try and hide rolling a joint on the table when the barmaid came to collect the glasses, and that's how you get barred for smoking dope in the pub, but if you just pull out a joint from your pocket and smoked it no one gives a shit. Well, it was OK back then before everyone went from smoking hash to grass. Skunk, now, will stink out the whole bar and the lounge with just one joint.

One time, Gerry told me his nephew who lived up in Inverness knew a guy who was selling a big lump of dope but he didn't want money for it - he wanted a gun. Gerry got an old cheap gun from someone in Glasgow and asked my dad to go with him. So they hit the road to Inverness. On the way they stopped off at Loch Ness. The sun was out and they wanted to take in all that the highlands had to offer so they sat at the loch having a joint. A dog walker went past and his big dog was off the lead. It ran over to my dad who is shit-scared of dogs so he said, "get that thing on its lead and away from me," and the guy laughed and said, "it won't hurt you". My dad retorted, "do you think its fucking funny," and pulled out the gun. The dog walker shits his pants grabbed his dog and ran faster than a fat guy trying to catch the curry shop before it shuts. Gerry told my old man to put that fucking thing away and get in the car. They headed a few miles up the road and a good few more, before stopping and going into a pub so my dad could get a drink. Inside the pub there were four young guys and two young girls. My dad and Gerry were sitting having a drink when an old homeless looking guy walked in. One of the young guys called him over and said you look hungry, and offered him some crisps. Just as the guy put out his hand to take them the young guy poured them out all over the pub floor. He said to the old guy, "well, what you waiting for, if you're hungry then eat them. No one's stopping you". Because the guy was hungry he did start to pick them up. All the young team were laughing. My dad looked at Gerry and Gerry said, "don't even think about it," but it was too late. My dad got up, walked over like a cowboy in the Wild West, pulled out the gun, showed it to the young guy who dropped the crisps and said, "why don't you get on your knees, ya wee fucker and eat them yourself. After all, you made the mess". The young guy started crying, and apologizing. My old man said, "buy the wee guy a drink to say sorry". By then, the whole pub was hiding under the tables but then big Gerry dragged my dad out of the pub into the car and told him, "that's it! No more stops till we get there."

Flannery... the Fla's were 5 brothers and one sister, Bernadette. Pat was the eldest of the brothers; he was my dad's pal. Well, over the years my dad was pals with a few of them but Pat was the first. Pat and my dad came up with the Oregon trail, which was a way to kill time away from the pub Yeah! you read that right. I said 'away from the pub'. You see, most of the guys in the Argosy had no family for all different reasons, like the wife had put them out for their drinking, or some guys never left home so whatever the reason they went to the pub all day and all night to kill a bit of time. What they would do was go to the off sales, get a bottle of Eldorado wine, or a litre (which was known as a fat lady) and they would walk over the railway bridge into Rosshall Park, sit by the River Cart, have a swig of wine and talk shit, then walk over the other bridge, which brought them out onto the streets just across from the pub. Everyone in the pub had done this for years. It was a good way to spend time away from the pub when the sun was out because the Argosy had no windows. It was like a Vegas hotel - they didn't want you to know what time it was. Some guys spend that much time in there when they walked out they were like vampires; I was waiting to see if they would burst into flames.

They say every man has a weakness. Well, Pat's was women. He loved the birds. My dad says he wouldn't have left Pat with my granny to make a cup of tea. His wee brother and my best pal, Chris Fla, says Pat had mad shaggers' disease. Pat, to me, was the guy who would be in the pub all the time but you would never see him drunk. He never got loud or made an ass of himself. I always liked that about him. He was always up for a chat and a good bit of banter. He was one of the cool guys in the pub and he knew how to talk to the females, which was good to watch and learn when you're a 15 year old kid, because at that age you don't know your asshole from your earhole, and when you try and talk to girls you just say the wrong thing and hang about them like a dog with a burst ball.

The second brother was Andy. He was a biker and got by doing a bit of money lending. Andy and my dad became drinking pals, I think because they were both splitting up with their wives at the same time. Andy was a good guy to know and a bad guy to have as an enemy. He didn't take shit from anyone and he would do anything for his family. He was old school - family first. He always had time for me as a kid he would get me a beer, ask me "how's things," and "if any one gives you a hard time, just you let me know". Andy was like a modern day cowboy; instead of a horse he had a motorbike, and as long as he had a drink and a few pals life was fine. Looking back now all these guys were rock and roll suicides, just living on the edge. Years ago in the pub the TV wasn't up on the wall - it was up in the corner of the pub on a shelf because they were big and bulky back then. Well, one day we were sitting having a beer and an old guy was sitting under the TV. Andy asked the old guy to move a wee minute so he could turn up the sound so the guys could hear the next race. Andy jumped back off the chair, the old guy sat back down and about twenty seconds later the TV fell off the wall and hit the old guy on the head, bang!!! It landed right on top of his head. I was sure the old chap was a goner. He must have thought the fucking pub had fallen down on top of him. We sat him up, asked him if he was OK, and once he opened his eyes, that is, he had a look around. He was fine. Well he was fine after Andy got him a beer and a half of whisky.

As much as Andy's life was upside down he always made time for his youngest brother, Chris. He would take him away for a few days up north, camping, and because I was Chris's pal I got to go, too. It was the best of times. I will never forget sitting at a campfire, drinking beer and looking at the night sky. Me and Chris never forgot about those weekends. We would talk about them for years to come and it was thanks to Andy that I love going up north, even after all the time that's passed. I can still remember Andy telling me and Chris, "don't waste your life sitting in a pub. Head out to the middle of nowhere, sit at a fire and enjoy your beer. Pubs are for old married men."

One night Andy and all his brothers were in the pub watching the football when a guy, Peter, whose second name I won't say, walked in. Peter and Andy had a run in with each other years back. Chris, Andy's youngest brother, noticed Peter walk in and sit at the back of the pub with a pint so Chris told Mark and they decided not to say anything to Andy, as they knew he would go over to dig him. So instead, they would just keep an eye on him. A few hours later Peter was walking past towards the pub door and as he passed Andy he pulled out a Stanley knife and ran it across his face. Chris told me the blood came out that fast it was spraying all over his face and it took a few seconds to work out what it was. Peter dropped the blade and ran for the door. Big John grabbed him and Peter pulled out another knife and stuck it in John's side, then he ran out the pub, over the road, jumped into a garden and hid behind the wall. One of Andy's brothers went out after him, looked over the wall and saw him lying on the grass. The brother pulled out his own knife, lent over the wall and stuck the blade in his side three or four times. He said Peter didn't move or make a sound as he stabbed him. After that he just walked back over to the pub to see how Andy and John were doing. Andy got stitches and was left with a scar on his face. Big John was OK, too; having a fat belly saved his life. Andy sadly passed away in 2005 with the drink. He was only in his fifties.

The day of his funeral my wife found out she was pregnant. I was waiting in the graveyard for Chris to make sure my pal was OK when he came over. We had a hug. I asked him how he was doing, then I told him I was going to be a dad again, and he said, "that's good mate, one door closes and another

one opens". My dad and Andy died the same year as each other
and that year me and my best pal, Andy's youngest brother,
Chris, talked a lot. We had lost our loved ones; the heartbreak
of losing a dad or a brother and these guys were our pals,
so we knew what each other was feeling and we would just
sit, get drunk and talk about old times. Me and Chris did the
Oregon trail one last time in 2005 in the middle of December;
it was cold and too wet to sit by the river but we stood on the
railway bridge with a bottle of wine. I kept saying, "I forgot
how good this tastes. Why did we stop drinking wine?" Well,
two bottles and eight pints of Guinness later I remembered
why: we stopped drinking it when my head was down the
toilet pan at 3 am.

Mick Fla was always laid back. Never in a hurry but always
on the go out of all the Fla's. Mick was the one who didn't
drink. He had his head screwed on. He was a punk back in the
day and played in a few punk bands all over the country. He
could also draw and was a really good artist. He was always
away, hill walking. Mick didn't need the pub he only went
because his brothers were all in there. He was happier away,
keeping fit and playing music and that's the best way to be
if you ask me. In the nineties he formed a rebel band, The
Claymores, and they sold out in all the Celtic pubs they played.

Rebel nights were no' my cup of tea because I wasn't into
football but I went to a few because my family and pals went
and most of the time it was Paddy's day so the Guinness was
always cheap. The one thing I did always think at those nights
was that I take my hat off to Mick; the guy was smart. He knew
how to make a few bucks without getting the jail for it like

most of the other guys in the pub, lending money or selling drugs. Thinking back now I loved Paddy's Night for cheap Guinness and we would go to any pub for a cheap pint or a free one no matter how rough it was. One night I was drinking with a guy from work and he said to me, "do you know how to get a free pint?" I was all ears. "No mate, how?" and he said, "watch this". We had both about less than half a pint left and he farted in his. Then said to the barmaid, "excuse me, hen, I think my beer is off". She smelled it and almost passed out. She was like, "Oh my God! that's off". Then she looked at me and said is yours the same?" I just nodded in shock, and she went and got us two full fresh pints. "Try them, lads." And my mate, Paul was like, "yeah, that's much better, thanks hen". That night I stood there thinking this guy is a genius; he should get awarded the Nobel peace prize.

The fourth brother, Mark Fla, was nicknamed Sharks... Sharks was the cool one of the brothers, always had fast cars, liked a good drink and a smoke and like Andy, you didn't want to get on the wrong side of him. Sharks wouldn't have words with a guy in the pub, then say, "right – outside!" No. If you had words with him and you made him feel uneasy then he would hit you and when you went down, best thing to do was stay down. If you were daft and got up and hit him back, then he would go for it. Sharks didn't take any chances; he was never going to lose a fight and if it wasn't finished with that night then he would wait two or three days and then get you on your way to work at 6am. That was the thing people didn't get - that if you were just out for a beer on your days off, don't get into a fight with any of the guys who were in the pub seven days a week. They don't give a fuck. If it's now Monday let's forget about it, I have work to go to now. No. They would come after you any day of the week and you would end up with a sore pair of balls and your P45 for fighting outside your work.

Looking back now I remember most of the money lenders would always be in the pub early on a Monday because they were out looking for the cunts who hadn't paid, get them while they still had a hangover. I liked having a drink with Sharks. He was the same as me. He didn't go to the pub to talk about football; no, we would talk about films, music, and take the piss out of everyone in the pub. Sharks was a truck driver and he would go all over the UK. He would let me and his brother Chris go with him sometimes, and we loved it. One night you would be in Inverness, then the next night down in Manchester. We would get cans of Coke, sandwiches and a few joints and just play music all night. Sharks was a big Rolling Stones fan just like me so I loved it. Sharks and my dad became pals as most of the Fla's were pals with my dad over the years. Sharks and my dad didn't sit and drink with everyone in the afternoon. No. He had a family, so after dinner he would head to the pub for a drink where my dad would be waiting on him, so everyone else would be away home and they would sit, drink, smoke and talk shit. They would drink so much whisky and smoke so much dope that if you popped in for a beer you knew just to leave them be. They were on another level and there was no keeping up with them, and at the end of the night they would walk home. I think Sharks liked to make sure my dad got home OK, what with my dad being older then him. They would walk the long road home, say good night, then Sharks would pop into the QV pub to have one more for the road, and they did that routine for years. Sharks doesn't go to the pub anymore because all his drinking pals are gone; all his mates were my mates, too, and they are all behind the sun now, and we miss them all really bad.

I met Shark's wife, Ann, not so long ago at the shops and she was in to get him a half bottle of Eldorado wine. She said he has one half bottle a week on a Saturday night, and I don't know why but that made me happy to know I wasn't the only one drinking a wine to our pals gone, but not forgotten. Hopefully they are all sitting in the city of gold drinking Eldorado and waiting on us to show up - well apart from my dad! He will no doubt be at an Elvis gig when I show up. Keep on trucking, Sharks. We are the last of the Mohicans.

Last but not least Chris Fla, my best pal and brother; Chris was all his brothers rolled into one. He looked up to them, what they said went as far as he was concerned. It was like he had four extra dads to look after him and keep him on the right path, no' a bad thing really. He was a punk, cool guy, artist and a loyal friend. I met Chris in the pub when he was 16 and I was 15. I had only been going to the pub a few weeks and my dad kept telling me to keep my head down, don't go to the bar and talk unless spoken to, because the guys in here don't won't to come in for a beer and hear what a 15 year old kid has got to say about life. So I stayed under the radar and did what I was told, because I didn't want to fuck up a good thing I had going by talking shit. Then one day this kid my age walks in, cool as you like, he had ripped jeans and a biker jacket on and

John Lennon specs. He went up to the bar, bought a bottle of beer and started talking away like he is 40 and had had a hard day at the office. And I'm hiding in the corner like Ann Frank. Mick Fla was no' too happy about his young brother being in the pub and said to my dad, "maybe Joe and Chris should meet and maybe become pals and we can get them to hang about away from the pub?" My dad agreed so Mick got Chris two bottles of beer and said, "one of them beers is for Joe. Go say hi". So over comes this cool dude, said, "hi I'm Chris, you want a beer?" I'm, like, "sure I'm Joe, nice to meet you".

We sat talking that day like we'd known each other for years and the plan worked. I went from not knowing many people in Penilee to running about with Chris, and he knew everyone. Every time the Eagles song, 'New Kid in Town' came on the radio he would always say, "that's you," even twenty years later. Chris's dad had a caravan out back that we would sit in getting drunk and stoned and we had an extension cable running from his bedroom window into the caravan so we could play our sounds and not piss off the neighbours. One morning after the night before I woke up and went for a piss and on my way to the toilet I saw a wee white pill on the floor. Then as I got to the back door of the house I saw another pill in the grass and all the way down to the back door. I walked into the kitchen to find Chris on the kitchen floor laid out like a cold buffet, still half-drunk, looking like his hangover was about to kick in. There was a wee pile of pills and a cigarette beside him he had been trying to light his cigarette with a packet of Sweetex.

Chris was the pal who got me into music. He had quite

some record collection from the sixties, seventies and eighties, the lot. We got stoned and listened to The Stones and The Who, even punk to Pink Floyd. All his pals owed him so many thanks for the music he introduced us to. His other favourite pastime was fighting and he never backed down from a fight. He made sure everyone knew he was a good guy but 'don't fuck with me'. Most times we got into a fight it would end with me pulling him off some guy on the ground trying to break it up. The one thing my dad always told me not to do was break up a fight because that's the guy who ends up getting punched or stabbed and he was right, but sometimes I had to break it up or the poor guy was going to hell, and Chris was going to jail.

Every Thursday me and Chris would go to the Argosy for a pub lunch and a few beers. I remember one particular day we had what we always had - cheese burgers and chips - but I was still feeling hungry afterwards and said, "I'm getting a sweet," and asked him if he wanted to get Black Forest gateau. Chris was like, "no, not for me, I'm keeping some room for the beer," and I'm like, "yeah, fuck it", so I ordered two. I ate all of mine but he only ate two bites of his and said, "I can't eat that. I'm full". Now Chris had a bit of a belly but it was a beer belly, no' a cake belly, but when you have a belly people think you're a greedy cunt, so when he went for a piss I thought 'fuck it, waste not, want not,' and swapped plates. I started to eat his cake but I had only had a few bites when I think, 'fuck this, I'm full, too' and left the rest.

The barmaid came over to take the plates away and her words were, "you all done here?"

"Yes thanks."

"You no' eating your cake?"

"No, I'm full, thank you."

And she then said, "your pal didn't half put a hole in his, didn't he?"

I didn't want to tell her that was my plate so I just said "yeah, he set about it all right,"

"No wonder he's so fat!" she replied.

Another big family was the Boyles: Shug, Mick, Gerry and Danny. I loved those guys. Over the years I hung about with them all. They were all great guys and all older than me so I respected the fact they made time to sit and have a beer with me. I mean, who wants to sit with a young kid who doesn't know shit about life yet? But the Boyles, like many of the guys in the pub, did. Maybe it was because of my dad, and they all knew and liked my brother Gerry so they made time for me. I was pals first with Danny. He had just split from his girlfriend and had a lot of time after work to think about it, so the best place to keep you busy from thinking too much was the pub. We would go up to the lounge on a Thursday night, me, Danny, my dad and maybe Mick Boyle, too. It was never busy on a Thursday, just a handful of people. We would play the jukebox game which was where we put in 25p each – four songs for a pound - and then see who could pick the longest running song, you know, get our money's worth. I would always go for midnight rambler by The Stones – it's about twelve minutes long. The best thing about that game was that some nights a couple would pop in for a few drinks and a chat and as they were sitting, maybe getting to know each other, the Doors song, 'The End' would come on. Fifteen minutes of Jim Morrison singing about the end of life and wanting to kill his father and fuck his mother! After that the couple would be off out the door.

Me and Danny smoked hash and drank cans of cider - they were a pound a can, a lot cheaper than a pint of beer. I mean, if you had £10 you were drinking ten cans. Happy days. Then they put the cans up to £1.50, the fuckers. Most of the guys were out of work so they would show up, have a few beers and then go home. Maybe if someone was in with a few bucks and got you another drink, then you could hang about, but you had to remember who did that for you so that when you were working and maybe they were out of work you could get them a drink in return. Mick and Shug Boyle were the most generous guys in the pub. They would always make sure you had a drink. Mick didn't work for years when I first met him, but when he got a job he would always make sure my dad had a beer when he was out of work; a true pal. When most of us were working times were good. We could afford to have a good time drinking and smoking on our weekends off.

Big Shug Boyle loved the riches in life. He would buy a bottle of red wine when everyone else was sharing Eldorado, but he worked all week so why not? I learned from Shug that there was more to life than sitting in the pub. If you work hard then you could go on holiday - sit in the sun or go up north, camping. We took my dad up to John O'Groats once and he said it was a fucking nightmare. Never again! But me and Shug loved it. The Boyles were everyone's pal but they didn't fuck about; they could all fight when they had to. Me, my dad,

Gerry and Shug were drinking one day and I went to get a round at the bar. A few guys were standing at the bar and I knew all of them apart from one who was laughing and talking loudly. As I asked for my drinks, one of them being a lager tops, the guy says, "are you drinking with your wife," and then starts laughing. I didn't click to what he meant till I sat down and by then I'm thinking, OK, he's making out a tops is a girls drink – whatever, let it go. But then Shug got up to get the next round, and as we were sitting there talking Shug hits the guy on the jaw, knocking him to the floor. As we all looked round and saw what was happening I guessed right away why Shug had hit him. But as the guys at the bar grabbed Shug, telling him to take it easy, it was a joke. The funny cunt is about to get back up, so I ran over, took a penalty kick to his head and it was night-night funny cunt. The boys picked him up and carried him out to a taxi and we took Shug back to the table. He still didn't know what the guy was talking about, just something about 'my wife's drink' and something about 'a cow', "so I hit him!" I told the boys it was my fault, he was making fun of me drinking lager tops, but my old man said, "well he's right, shandy is for kids".

There were loads of other mad and lovable characters in the pub, like I said: John Bonnie and Rab Donnelly, Mick Reid and many more. My dad told me about the time him and all the boys went to John's when his mum and dad were away on holiday. He got the boys up for beers and food and put on a dirty video. They drank and smoked all night. He got up the next morning to all the mess: the dishes were all over the place, empty beer cans, whisky bottles and hungover bodies.

He didn't know where to start so he put the dishes in the shower and washed them and himself at the same time. John must have been in his thirties when I first met him. I was told that when he was about 18 he had a girlfriend, his first love and best pal. One hot summer's day they went away for the day in his dad's car; on the way there they were in a bad accident and when John came out of a coma a few weeks later he was told his girlfriend had died at the scene and that's when I think John found the House of the Rising Sun AKA the Argosy Bar, because when you can't move on you hide away, and the best place to hide is the pub. Leave your troubles at the door, come in, sit down, have a beer or a half or both, talk about good times or bad, but the main thing is you have a laugh. And that's why we go to the pub to start with, until the drink gets a hold of you, then that's you - a full member.

The thing I think my dad and his pals liked about the Argosy was it didn't matter what day or time you went in for a drink, there was always someone in the corner you knew. You never went in and had a beer alone;, the corner had the day time drinkers, and the night time drinkers, and the weekend guys who worked Monday to Friday, so you always had someone to have a beer and a bit of banter with to help forget your troubles. My dad was known as Tash. He was a die-hard Elvis fan and made it his goal in life to turn everyone into liking the king. My dad's routine was like he was in jail - everything he did at the same time - you could set your clock by it day in and day out. He would go to my gran's in the morning, make sure she was OK (but really him showing up was letting my gran know he was OK). He would have a cup

47

of tea, some food and sit in the kitchen and do the crossword. He was never in a hurry to go to the pub and I was always thinking 'hurry the fuck up, let's get a beer', but he'd been doing this routine for years and all the fun was gone; the same old shit, day in and day out. His flat was a wee one room shithole; he called it Fort Sedgewick from the film 'Dances with Wolves'. He wouldn't buy food to cook; he would just go to the chip shop. I could never understand why he lived the way he did but looking back over the years I think he was punishing himself for losing his wife and sons to the drink, and it was too late to fix it now, so let's just keep on drinking till the big man in the sky says time's up.

When he was in the pub my dad would hold court; he knew how to tell a story – fuck, he could talk about just going to the shops to put the lottery on and everyone in the corner would sit and listen. All the guys had a routine outside the pub with work or family, but they all lived for the pub. I'm amazed that some of them are still alive, like my old pal, Mick Reid, is still going strong into his seventies. But Mick was old school like my old man. They drank beer and I mean real beer, like Tartan Special or Guinness and tonic wine which in moderation is good for you, no' like today's young team, all drinking dragon soups and shots - good luck growing old drinking that shit. The guys back in the day were all strong, big lads because they worked hard and drank beer and if a fight kicked off you were best out the way of it. They all had hands like stone; one fist was dynamite and the other fist was goodnight. and as I said before, my old man always says don't break up a fight, let them get on with it because the guy who splits it up always gets a smack in the eye for his thanks. And some of the guys didn't fuck about with punches, they carried a blade so you didn't want to be in the middle of that fight. My dad learned that one the hard way. One day when Rab D set about some loud drunk stranger, the two of them were rolling about under a table and my dad stepped in to split it up before Rab killed the guy, but his leg got in the way and Rab stabbed him.

I asked my dad, "did Rab D say sorry?"

and he said, "well yeah, sort of.

I said, "what do you mean, sort of?" and he said, "he got me a bottle of Eldorado the next day".

There was not one bad guy in the pub back then, a few mad ones like The Claw, a wee drunk guy who would grab with his hand like a claw, or old Murphy - he was a school teacher but then his wife left him for another guy and he had a breakdown and hit the drink. He would sit and talk to himself about how you should never break anyone's heart and he would just sit all day going on and on. I got a job working in a Levendale, a psychiatric hospital, and I knew most of the patients. They drank in the pub. All of my dad's pals would let me sit with them but they didn't want me getting drunk because of my age, except for Mick Reid. I loved having a drink with Mick and still do. He wouldn't give a shit once he had a few beers. He loved beer and horses. If he got a winner he would say, "Joe, son, get the beers in," and when he had a hangover he would always say, "I need a rub down, 'Deed I Doo'.

The first time I met Mick I was about ten and my dad had

told my brother to bring me to the pub as he and a few of his mates would take us swimming. Me, my dad and Gerry were going for a swim and his pals were going for a jacuzzi and sauna. As we stood outside the pub waiting to go Mick Reid walked up. "All right boys, what's happening?" he said. One of the boys said, "we're going for a jacuzzi. You fancy it?" and Mick says, "no thanks, I don't like Chinese". For years after that I would always ask Mick if he wanted a Jacuzzi and rice for his dinner.

Even the local priest who drank in the pub was a good guy - Father Jim. He would pop in every Friday night for one beer while he was waiting on his curry getting made. He said he was hooked on curry sauce like we were hooked on Coke. He would always get me a beer and never take one back. Every time I would say, "right Jim, you want a pint?" and he would shout, "no, I'm off. I will pray for you," as he ran out the door. One time I asked him if he could sign my passport forms and he said, "sure, bring them to the chapel house," so I popped in with them. His maid or whatever you would call her let me in and asked me to wait in the kitchen. The house was so big inside, the kitchen was bigger than my flat. Jim came in with a tracksuit on and said "alright, Joe? You want a beer?" and I'm like, "sure Father".

We sat at this big breakfast bar and I said, "this is all a bit much for just one guy, is it no'?"

And Jim said, "yeah, it's normally two priests, but it's just me now".

I asked him, "did you like having another priest to share with," and he said, "no, it's a pain in the ass. When I first moved in an old priest was here and one day I came back from the shop, made myself a sandwich and a cup of tea and I put the sandwich down on the work top. I went over and poured my tea, sat down with the paper and when I took a bit of my sandwich it was wet and I'm thinking why is the bread wet? The work top was dry so I just carried on eating my wet sandwich and drinking my tea while reading my paper when the old priest walked into the kitchen and said 'excuse me I need to get my underwear down from the pulley'...

I was like, "no way,"

and Father Jim said, "yeah the old git had put his smelly old pants on the pulley and they were dripping into my sandwich. So when he left the first thing I did was decorate the kitchen and got the pulley taken down".

I told him the last party I was at in the Argosy the couple must have been skint because the buffet was a loaf of bread a tub of butter and a packet of meat on each table.

Jim didn't believe me. He said, "no way,"

and I'm like, "I would never lie in God's house. I swear when I walked into the party my pals were looking where to sit so they got a packet of meat that they liked".

It was a make your own sandwich buffet and the good thing was you didn't need to wait for the DJ to tell you the buffet was open but you did need to make your sandwich before 9pm so they could collect all the butter knives back before everyone got drunk and a fight kicked off. The last thing you need is the pub full of butter knives.

The first time I met Jim he was blessing the coffin I was

carrying and I had on a pair of black snakeskin shoes. My wife told me I couldn't wear them to a funeral but I was thinking 'yes I can, they look cool'. So as father Jim passed by me, throwing his holy water everywhere he said to me, "what's the story about your shoes, big man? That's no' right wearing them at a funeral". I swear everyone carrying the coffin heard him. I could feel them all laughing.

There was also a lot of really intelligent guys in the pub, too, because alcohol and drugs will get a hold of you no matter how rich or poor you are. There were teachers who had hit rock bottom on the drink because their marriages were over, and other guys who had been doing good in life and then one day a bit of bad luck happened to them, and they would never get over it so they would hide away in the pub and let time slip on by. One of the guys who was like this was Big Neil. He seemed out of place in the Argosy - a very well-spoken, big guy and very intelligent, too, so when I first met him I couldn't work out why he wasn't sitting in some bar in town talking the talk with some chums. But as my old man had told me, all the guys were in here for pretty much the same thing - hiding from a woman, and that was the same for Neil. His wife had left him and took his two young kids, and he was living in a wee shithole of a flat and passing his time in the pub. Neil went from being very clever to being too close to the edge; you know when they say there is a fine line between genius and madness, well, that's where his life had taken him. He would say to me, "my neighbours give me a hard time so to piss them off I wash their windows with soft boiled eggs". I would think 'what the fuck are you about' but I was too young to know the guy was losing his mind, trying to get over losing his family. All I knew was my old man looked out for Neil the best he could. He would tell him to take it easy with the drink and the dope. Another thing Big Neil would do was to pick an argument with guys like Gerry Law or Rab Fraser, like he had some sort of death wish, but Gerry and Rab would let it go because they knew my old man would dig Neil up and have a word with him.

Back then in the nineties I would come in for a beer playing my Walkman and all the guys would want a listen, and big Neil loved it. I would have a tape in it - side one, The Rolling Stones and side 2, Elvis for my dad. So whenever my old man was finished I would hand it over to Neil so he could listen to the Stones and he loved it .He would shout the lyrics back to me like I was in my basement room with a needle and a spoon and another girl to take my pain away!! And I would be like, "yeah, OK mate, keep it down," but he would be off, lost in the moment. Neil came and went from the pub over the years and a lot of the guys didn't have any time for him except me and my old man, but as I said he didn't do himself any favours. He would always get into an argument with someone. There was no talking to him; like if Rab Fraser said something funny, Neil would shout or laugh. I nearly died, and Big Fraser would go fucking nuts at him. I knew it was just a matter of time before Rab would set about him. He was asking for it for years and it was only because my old man would ask Rab to let it go that he did. All the time I would ask my dad about it and he would say Neil was winding Rab up again last night, and I would tell my old man, "look, when Rab goes for him you need to stand back and let it happen. It's been coming for a long time".

And after all the years of Neil and Rab no' seeing eye to eye, it finally happened. That night my old man, Neil, Chris and Mark Fla were sitting drinking. They were well on it, been in most of the day, when Rab walks in needing a drink. He had had a rough week with one of his kids in hospital so as you can imagine, he wasn't in the best of moods and Neil went for it. Rab warned him, "not tonight, pal" but Neil and his death wish didn't give up, so words were going back and forth till it was Neil who offered Rab outside. I'm sure he was the only idiot to ever invite Rab outside for a square go. My old man tried to stop it but Neil kept on. Even Rab tried to tell him. "If I start hitting you, the way I'm feeling I won't stop," but still Neil went for him. Rab punched him once and down he went. He almost killed him that night. My old man dragged Rab off him and the staff phoned for an ambulance, and after that we never saw Neil again. He never came back. Years later I was talking to Rab about it and he said, "the cunt was asking for it" and I said, "yeah, he had a death wish. I think he couldn't face suicide so he tried to get you to do his dirty work".

JOHN WAYNE
AT NIGHT,
BIG WAYNE IN
THE MORNING.

CHAPTER 3

Pub Stories

Everyone these days loves to have a day out on a Sunday; even better if they are off on the Monday. In Glasgow they call it a 'Sunday sesh' and when I was a you kid back in the day Sunday was always a busy day in the pub; everyone you knew was in and they were all there to cure their hangovers. Sunday was the day that you played games like darts, pool and dominoes. I liked dominoes the best; darts was hard work, trying to subtract was a killer for me. My dad was a big fan of darts, he could subtract really fast and he would get pissed off when I couldn't do it. Everyone would be waiting and he would say, "we don't have all day," and I would say, "yes you do because you cunts don't have anywhere better to be". The best tip I got for playing dominoes was from Big Shug Boyle. He told me that when you get the double six stick it in some cunt's pint of Guinness. Shug was a great big guy. He was my dad's pal from when they were kids and he became my best pal in the pub. I was pals with his brother Danny at first; you see, with a pub you become pals with a guy because you're maybe going through the same shit in life so if you split up with a bird you go to the pub to drink your troubles away and who do you find in the pub? Danny was going through the same shit, so you get drunk together.

I was pals with all the Boyles; everyone got on with them. Such good guys, but they were no one's mugs. I never saw any of them lose a fight. On a Sunday there was anything between ten to fifteen guys, all in the corner and all of the Fla's and Rab Donnelly at the corner of the bar. All of the session ticket holders who got the Celtic bus to the game would fill the place. And there was a table full of all the gamblers, and the most famous gambler was George Harvey. I have never seen anyone bet like he did and I don't think I will ever see anyone like that again. The first time I got to know George he came into the pub and got me and my dad a drink. He told my dad him and his wife were buying a house; it was twenty grand and his wife, for some mad reason, let him go to the bank to pick up the money. So as he passes our drinks over to us he tells us he has lost ten grand already. My dad went, "fucking hell George! What you going to do? She'll kill you". He said, "I'm going back to win it back, and if I don't get it back I 'll stop at two grand, go to the airport and get a flight to Canada and stay with my brother till she gets over it and it's safe to come home. So a few hours later George comes back into the pub buys a large drink and says to the barmaid, "get Arthur and his son a drink and phone me a taxi for the airport, hen". He downed the drink and walked out the door and stayed in Canada for a few weeks till the dust settled.

I never got into gambling, thank fuck, and as my old man always said, you can only drink so much, then you'll be sick, but you can gamble your life away in a day and I watched a lot of guys do just that. If I put £5 on a horse and it lost I was gutted and would think 'fuck that, never again!' but some of the guys would lose their whole week's wage on a Friday. I could never work it out why you would do that to yourself and your family. I walked in one day and Rab and George were down £1000 each so they did a deal with the bookie for a horse in the next race - if it won they wouldn't owe the bookie anything but if it lost they would owe him two grand each - and the bookie OK'd it. When the race started Rab and George went outside for a smoke. They didn't want to watch it, but I did and the horse came in second place. I was like, holly shit! Rab will beat up the whole pub, and a few of the guys in the pub were saying to me go you tell him; he won't hit you, you're like a son to him. And I was like, "yeah a step-son, so fuck off and tell him yourself".

I walked in one Saturday night about six and got a beer and as I looked around I saw one of the gamblers, Liam, sitting studying the TV. Liam is younger than me but was right into gambling. He was a really good guy to get on with like most of the gamblers; when they win they let it be known it's party time.

So anyway, I sit down and say, "alright?" and asked him if he wanted a beer.

He said, "no thanks mate, and if this horse in the next race comes in I'm buying the beers".

I said," and if it doesn't ?"

He replied, "well my Saturday night will be drinking tea and watching the X factor with my mum".

The horse didn't come in!

Right I think it's about time I bring Rab Fraser into the

party. He was, and still is, my best mate and my drinking buddy for thirty years. We had many a good weekend together. I remember me and Rab waiting for the pub to open one Sunday. We were banging on the door telling the barmaid to hurry up and get the doors open, the drink is flowing like mud out here. We got in, drank all day, everyone coming and going and me and Rab still drinking, and at the end of the night when the last orders' bell rang we were the last two left, and the staff were telling us that it was time to go home. When I first went into the pub in 1991 Rab was in jail. He had got into a fight with a few guys in the snooker club around from the Argosy. He left the club and went to the pub to get out of the way. He knew if he was to hang around he would end up in the jail that night, but two of the guys turned up at the pub trying to keep it going. Maybe they were thinking because they were drunk they could set about him, but it didn't go as planned for them. When Rab saw them at the door it was like a red rag to a bull. He went for them, dragged them out into the street, and set about doing what he did best. The two so called hard men stuck him in big time and he got a few years in jail. Years later we were in the pub and one of those guys came in for a drink and he almost got a sip of it, when Rab saw him. Rab said, "take one sip of that beer and you're a dead man". The guy put the drink down and walked out and never came back.

I had been going to the pub for about a year and Rab was getting weekend release so on a Sunday he would want a skin full before he would head back that night. Rab was in Greenock jail. My dad and Rab Donnelly would go there to visit him. They came back one day and told us they had found a shop that sold orange wine; everyone in the pub was a wine drinker so they all wanted to try this wine. Turns out it was Mad Dog 20/20 and it showed up in Glasgow about a year later, and still gets drunk to this day by all the young team, and they call it 'a bottle of dug'. Me, I'm just like my old man, I'm an Eldorado drinker. When Rab got out of jail we became best pals. I mean, he was my dad's pal and he was pals with my brother, Gerry, but with me, I think the reason we got on so well was that I would take the piss out of him and he loved it. No one else would do it and for good reason. They wouldn't get away with it. But I was much younger, so I could. It was like he would be digging someone up and I would say to the guy, "he just dug. Are you taking that off him?" The poor guy would be like, "Joe, shut the fuck up, please".

Rab was the only guy back then to bring his wife to the pub. No other guy ever did this and to be fair most of them were in the 'my baby left me club'. The pub got done up once and my mum asked me if it was nice inside. I said it was OK, but you don't want it to be nice, and my mum asked me why no'. I said, "well, if it's nice women would want to drink in it. Rab would come in with his wife, Jackie, or as my dad called her, Peter. They would come in, get the drinks in and sit down beside me, and then within a few minutes Rab would say he needed a piss, then just head to the bar and leave me sitting talking to Peter, his wife.

I would give it about ten minutes, then go to the bar for a drink and ask him, "did you forget something?"

"No," he would say with a big smile on his face,

and I would hit out with, "if I wanted to talk to a bird I would have stayed home and got a few cans. Now come and get Peter. She is busting my ears about grandkids".

I still love sitting having a beer with Rab. He's never changed after all these years. He's still nuts and still funny, and he's never let old age slow him down. He'd been in hospital, got the big C, but got a day pass out to go to a funeral. After the funeral he was in the pub with me drinking and I'm trying to tell him, "you've just had a major operation, mate, slow it down," but he was like, "just a few more drinks, then I will go back. Joe". The old school guys are made of hard stuff I think if it wasn't for their drink and drugs they wouldn't have all made it into their nineties.

One Christmas Eve I walked into the pub and Rab was fighting with two young guys. He was standing on one of them, his foot on the guy's neck, and had his hands around the other one's throat.

I walked up and said, "merry Christmas. What's happening?"

and he came back with, "lads were a wee bit cheeky".

I said, "lads, he'll let you go and you will get to fuck out of here and have a merry Christmas, OK?"

He let them go and they ran faster than Rudolph.

A really good game to play when the pub was busy was 'change the channel' when Celtic and Rangers were playing; that was a good but really dangerous game. Apart from football being more important than life itself, a lot of the guys had serious money betting on the game, so if I got my hands on the remote I would change the channel, then chuck that remote away like it was a live grenade. The other good game to pass the time was to shout on guys as they walked out the door, then go back to drinking your beer and watch from the top of your pint glass for them looking about to see who was shouting on them. I loved this game; it was sick but funny as fuck, and when you think about it most of these guys were drunk and thinking that someone was shouting them back for another beer. A wee guy named Joe fell for it all the time. He went to the manager to get us barred so we were told to cut it out or we would be barred. So one Sunday wee Joe was heading for the door and we all looked at each other. My dad said, "don't fucking do it". Gerry and Rab looked at me like 'fuck it, do it'. The wee guy put his hand on the door and I shouted, "Joe!" He turned back for a look around, then looked at us and headed over. He said, "you lot are nothing but big fucking kids. Away and grow up. You're not funny and should be ashamed of yourselves". We all sat with our heads down in shame, he turned with his head high and walked away but as he got to the door and put his hand on it, I shouted, "Joe!!!!" The poor wee guy just shook his head and walked out.

Me and Rab would meet on a Sunday. His mum and dad owned the biggest house in Crookston but they had both passed away over the years. At the time we were meeting Rab and his brothers sold the house and split the money. Rab had his share under the bed. he couldn't put it in a bank because it would show up on the taxman's radar so every Sunday he would walk down the Crookston Road, phone me as he was outside my flat, and say, "you OK boy? It's time for a beer". A few times I would say, "no' the day, mate," but he would just go, "don't start your shit. I don't care if you're skint. I have money so move," and I would be ready anyway. We would walk down the road, have a catch up about the night before, then hit the pub all day. I will never forget the guys like Rab and all the others who got me a drink when I was skint - real pals.

My dad only went to the pub six days a week. I know that sounds bad - only six - but on a Saturday he would spend the day with his brother, Joe. I would go in on my days off through the week, and the gang would sometimes say, "your old man's no' been in for a few days which most of the time ment he had gout. He had suffered with if for a few years and would have to stop drinking for three or four days. I would go up to his flat to see how he was. Now you could set your watch by my dad. As I said before he worked on time, and he did the same things day in and day out - like in the morning he would go to the shop for a paper and two rolls, and keep them for the next day. You know, like he would get up, read his paper eat his rolls and have a cup of tea. That way if he woke up with gout and couldn't get to the shops he would at least have 2 rolls and a paper for the day anyway. But one morning he got up and his foot was killing him. He knew the gout was kicking in; it was in the post, as they say, and that meant he wouldn't be able to get out of the house for a few days. My dad says gout is like walking barefoot over broken glass so he was thinking 'I better get to the shops and get the food supplies in for the next few days, stay off the drink and sweat it out'. So he headed into the wee shop and the guy behind the counter grabs his paper and two rolls.

My dad said, "make it four rolls today,"

to which the guy said, "oh, sounds like someone has company".

My dad replied, "yeah I pulled a young bird in the pub last night and I'm giving her a dry roll and tea with no milk or sugar, because I know how to treat a woman right".

There was always someone missing in the pub whether it was from being skint, having gout or a hangover, jail or rehab – well, back then jail was rehab. Some of the guys hardest part of the day was just getting to the pub for a drink to chase away the shakes. If you were in early just after opening time you would see the guys getting a pint and a half and the barmaid or a pal carrying it to the table so they didn't spill it. I mean they were shaking that bad, if they carried it themselves it would have been empty by the time they sat down. When these guys walked past me I would stick my pint glass under their drink to catch it. Better in my beer than on the old pub carpet.

One weekend me, Gerry and Rab were having a drink when a wee guy we all knew from Penilee walked in for a beer. I won't say his name because I know his wife, so we shall call him Bob. So Bob sat down, asked us how we are all doing, and I asked him, "how's things?" "Great," he said. "I'm working down in London six weeks on, then three weeks off, but I tell the wife I'm down in London for seven weeks, so on the last week me and the guys I work with go to Bangkok to get drunk and fuck lady boys.... just like that he hits out with it, like it was no big deal. I was in shock... "Bob what the fuck!!!" He said, "well me and the wife don't have sex anymore and the lady boys are cheap". Then he tells us his last trip away

65

they took a young guy away with them. He was only nineteen and had never been outside the UK before. He said when they landed at the airport, a mini bus picked them up and they told the young guy, "when we get to the hotel they'll take our bags away so we can go right to the pool for food and beer. And while we drink our cold beers in the hot sun the girls who are at the pool will suck our dicks but when they are done we all tip our girl £5 each". So this young guy gets a beer and a BJ sitting by the pool, thinking best holiday ever. Later on at the bar Bob asked the lad if he was enjoying his holiday so far. "Yeah I am, but there's just one thing. After that BJ I gave the girl her £5 and as I said thanks I rubbed her chin and she had stubble". And Bob said "yeah! What the fuck do you want for a fiver?" We all sat there speechless for the first time ever. No one had anything to say. We just looked lost and old Bob was like, "what? Did I say something wrong?"

Around about 1997 the bar in the pub shut for a week; they had a film crew in for the film 'Acid House'. In the film the guy meets God and guess where God is sitting? In the pub in my old man's seat. They opened the lounge for us that week and it was like we went back in time when up the lounge was busy. I loved it, my dad and Gerry, not so much. We sat up at the window out of the way so we could smoke our hash and not let anyone smell it. The bar being shut really put them out of their routine, but up at the window was a wee bit to sit out of the way, where no one could see us so we all sat there, and one day Gerry and my dad were talking about music and my dad, said he loved the song by the Proclaimers, 'Sunshine on Leith'. So Gerry said to me, "go put it on the jukebox" which I did. We sat there stoned, and listened to it. At the end Gerry said to my dad, "yeah, that's a great song, Tash," and then says to me, "go put it on again". I think they got me to play it about six times because they were all stoned; they could just sit all day. The rest of the pub could hear it but they could only see me going back and forth to the jukebox so they were all thinking I'm sitting up there all alone playing sad songs, missing some wee bird and feeling sorry for myself. When I went to the bar the barmaid said, "you have a few pints in the tap. Guys were buying a beer and saying put one in the tap for young Joe, poor kid. Acid house was an OK film. Think it was trying to live up to Trainspotting at the time, but what would have made it an even better film was if they got the guys from the pub to be the extras. Fuck me that would have been class! To watch it now would be like watching some old wedding videos and some of the extras would have been more fun to watch than the main stars of the film. Yeah, shame. They missed a trick there.

You were never safe in the pub and when you were drunk someone would always play a joke on you. Like one day old Brian, a regular in the pub, went to get his messages, some food shopping and then walking home on what was a sunny afternoon, decided to pop in for a cold beer. But he was telling himself just the one, then get home and get the food in the fridge. Well that didn't happen because Brian was a greedy fuck on the drink so he got shit-faced drunk, passed out, and when I walked in the poor guy had shorts on, and someone had gone into his shopping bag, took out the cucumber he had bought, and stuck it up his shorts. Imagine the barmaid's face when she went to clean the table. The poor old cunt! One minute you're doing your shopping, getting by in life, then the next thing you know you're shit-faced with vegetables down your pants. And he got barred that day, too, for mistaking the manager's office for the toilets. Poor guy! He was as much use as a cock-flavoured lollipop.

Everyone loves a good story and bit of goss,' and sitting in the pub with a beer is the best place to hear or tell one. I remember as a young kid sitting with my dad and this guy walks in who knew my old man from years ago. They got talking and he told us he had split up with his wife but was loving single life. Then he said he was out at the weekend, up at the plaza, which is an old ballroom in Glasgow. He said he met this really nice woman and had a talk and a wee dance with her. At the end of the night he made sure she got home safely; they got a taxi to her flat where she asked him if he would like to come in for a nightcap. He said they had a few glasses of wine and she had this lovely big dog, a golden Labrador that sat beside him the whole time . So I'm sitting there taking all this in, thinking 'that's good, this guy has found love again.' But then he hits out with the last part of the night - he says she put the dog away in the room so they could have a kiss on the sofa, then he tells my dad, "next thing I know, Arthur, is I had her bent over the sofa and she is saying 'fuck me hard, take me from behind' and while I was giving her one her big dog walked back into the room and started to sniff my ass, and then it licked my balls". My dad says, "fucking hell did you get a fright," and the guy says, "get a fright! No, it was the best ride I have ever had....". And that's the great thing about people talking in a pub. You don't know where the story is going, good or bad funny or sad.

I remember having a beer with old John Smith. The guy was about 71 years old. We were sitting drinking on a Thursday afternoon at about half past one when this old couple walked in. The old guy tells his wife to get a seat and he goes to the bar. She sits at the table beside me and old John. She is soaked to the bone so you can tell its pissing down outside, and we know it has been all morning.

John says to her, "is it raining out there?"

and the old lady says, "yes it is."

So John says, "it wasn't raining when I came in,"

and she says, "really? When did you come in?" "Tuesday!!"

That was the way old John was. he couldn't help himself. He had to fuck with people. If a guy was sitting reading the paper he would ask him what time was the midnight movie on at? I think he was the first guy I ever met with Tourette's. He couldn't sit still, and would laugh out loud for no reason. And when he was sitting with a few of us having a drink and some dickhead would walk in, he would shout out 'hello' to them, and most of the time the dickhead would get a beer and come over to sit down. Then old John would get uneasy because he knew he had fucked up and the minute this dickhead went for a piss we would be letting him know big time, so the old cunt would get off, right out the door - bye! And leave us sitting with some dick talking about his shit life.

The only guy I knew who didn't accept the dickhead, the shit-talkers, the ear busters was Chris Fla. He was ruthless with them. He didn't give them a minute. As soon as some guy went to start talking about his new car or new job Chris would just shout out, "boring!!!" The whole pub would look round it was that loud, and he would do it to females, too. No one escaped. It was a killer. I mean, none of us were Brad Pitt and as my old man always said, if any of us fell into a barrel full of tits we would come out sucking our thumb. So whenever I was talking to some birds and trying to make them think I really wanted to hear all about them, I would be praying Chris, who was standing beside me drinking, wouldn't shout out "boring!!" One time we were talking to two, sisters and Chris says to the one I liked, "you look like someone I used to work with," and the girl says, "yeah, what was her name?" Chris says, "I didn't say it was a she...".

The only good thing about trying to get a bird in the Argosy was because most of the punters had a really bad drink or drug problem it wasn't hard to be the best looking guy in the pub. So if some bird did wander in off the street you could most likely be the best of a bad bunch. I got talking to a bird once in the pub and the next day Chris says, "that wee bird had some pair of tits, mate," and I said, "she had a Wonderbra on," and he says, "what do you mean?" I said, "they call it a Wonderbra because when you take it off you wonder where they fucking went, mate".

I was at the bar one night getting a round of drinks in and suddenly all the old guys in the pub were there all buying cans of Holsten Pils. Now a few things stood out about this one - 1 not one of these old fuckers drank Holsten Pils, 2 it was known as a woman's drink, it even had a nickname 'leg opener', and 3 why were they all of a sudden buying it just now? Even the barmaid knew but when I got back to my table my old man and the rest of the boys had worked it out - it was some old dear had come into the pub and sat down with the old guys up in the other corner from us and as she got talking to one of them she basically told him, "if you buy me a can you can shag me, and that goes for everyone". This old guy, Tam, was first to get her a can and she just pulled up her old kilt and dropped her city slickers. Old Tam went in for the kill faster than a junkie going for methadone. The barmaids got wind of what was going down and ran over telling Old Tam to get off of her and he was barred. Guys were shouting, "leave it out, the last time he got his end away the Beatles were at number one". The pub was in an uproar, the barmaids were going nuts and we were all pissing ourselves. The old dear got told to go, and she just pulled up her city slickers and said, "right boys, see you round the back, and don't forget the Holstens". My dad was like, "fucking hell, that's no' right. She's some cunt's granny, she should be in the house making fucking soup, no' out drinking super lagers". We were all falling about laughing.

The next day was Old Firm day so the pub was always busy. Everyone would show up and as much as I wasn't a big football fan I would show up, too. It was good sitting with all the boys; I could handle football for ninety minutes as long as the beer and the banter was flowing, and it always was. Just as the game was about to start I would shout, "come on Rangers, let's get into them!!" Everyone in the pub would have the look to kill in their eye, looking to see who the fuck shouted that, then see it was me and just laugh. Apart from my dad, that is. He would always say, "it's no' funny so don't do it," and I was like, "when Big Gerry does it, it's funny," and he would say, "well, let him do it then, no' you!" "OK Pops, chill."

My first Old Firm game in the pub was madness. I was looking forward to it for weeks. We sat in the opposite corner so we could see the TV. Everyone squeezed in with one another to see the TV, all drinking and smoking dope. In the second half Celtic were winning 2 – 1. The pub was going nuts. Everyone was singing and the staff were telling them to shut up, but they just kept going. So the manager shouted, "if you don't stop singing the TV is going off". Still no one was giving a fuck; they were all still going for it and me, this 16 year old kid, I'm just sitting in the middle of it like I was lost at sea. So the manager gets a chair to stand on to turn the TV off because some cunt has hidden the remote. As she gets on the chair she looks like she's on a fucking tight-rope trying to reach up to the button to turn it off, and someone shouts, "she's going to do it," and Big Gerry who is sitting beside me rolling a joint looks up, sees what she's about to do. He picks up my beer glass and throws it at her. It shot by her head like in slow motion, just missing her by a bawhair. It landed and smashed all over the tiled floor. She looks round still holding on to the TV shelf and shouts to the barmaids, "look and see who doesn't have a pint, they're getting barred". So I'm the only cunt without a beer I'm thinking 'great, I'm just in the pub and now I'm about to be barred for life'. As I'm sitting there with all the staff running around looking for the suspect I can see all the boys don't know what to do here. I'm thinking 'shit, I'm on my own here', then I looked to the guy beside me who is that drunk he has fallen asleep, so as the staff come running over I grab his pint and cool as you like I slide it over beside me. My dad and all the boys burst out laughing as the staff grab the sleeping drunk and shout to the manager, "we've found him". I was off the hook by the skin of my teeth, just. The poor guy was put out and barred for life before he had even woken up. His brother was at the bar and saw what had happened and came over to dig me up, but before I could say anything Gerry told him to fuck off, and the guy went, "but Gerry, he's getting barred for life," and Gerry just said, "I told you to fuck off".

I came into the pub late one day and the Celtic and Rangers game had already started, and the pub was that busy I decided to just stand at the bar and wait till half time before I would get a seat in the corner. As I was sipping my cold beer three guys walked in and ordered up three cans of Coke and then asked the barmaid to turn the TV over to Channel 2 as the cricket was on. You should have seen her face! She was looking at the three guys, who were all Muslim, thinking this must be some kind of joke, but it wasn't. I was standing there with the beer in my mouth looking, and thinking 'I hope to fuck she does it'. She told them, "I can't turn it over because the game is on and it's Celtic and Rangers playing," so one of them says, "look, we're paying customers and have a right to ask for the cricket to be put on". By now I'm thinking this is going to be so good. Hope to fuck she turns it over; the pub will turn into the Wild West, but she didn't. She told them, "for your own safety take your money back and go and watch it at home".

That day my dad's cousin, Spud, had showed up. I

remember Spud from when I was a wee kid; he was like our uncle, and a good one at that - always having a laugh with us. I was happy to see he hadn't changed one bit. We sat having a few beers. Spud and my dad were best pals back when they were kids, always getting up to no good. Spud told me him and my dad went to visit family down south for a few days and one night in their uncle's house they had a party. Everyone from down south came to the one house to have a drink with Spud and my dad, and when they got up in the morning Spud told my dad that he had pissed the bed.

My old man, raging, told Spud, "you better go down and tell them, and say fucking sorry," so he did, and on the way home on the train my dad asked him how did they take the bad news about pissing the bed?

Spud said, "OK, I think".

My dad asked, "were you embarrassed?" "

No," said Spud, "I told them you'd pissed it".

Another good friend who was in that day was Donny Brown. Donny was always on the move. He could sing and play the guitar so he would just move around busking all over Europe. He didn't take drugs, he just drank beer, but every man has a weakness and his was gambling. I drank with Donny on and off for years. If he wasn't around we would just think, 'well he'll be busking somewhere for money'. I had a lot of time for Donny. He was one of the good guys. Around about 2002 we hadn't seen him for a while and my dad told me he had been arrested for bank robbery. I couldn't believe it! Donny was no bank robber. He didn't even get into fights in the pub, but from what we had been told he had moved to Paisley to get out of the way of the boys in the pub he had borrowed money from but only went and got in deep with moneylenders he didn't know in Paisley. And these guys were no' fucking about, and told him to pay back what he owed within a week, or else. My poor mate Donny had no way out so he robbed the bank and got four years for it. A few years after he got out he told me about it. He said he was so nervous that when he walked into the bank he was so busy shaking that when he went to pull down his mask he dropped the gun and then when he went to pick it up he fucking kicked it. By the time he got the gun and had stood up and shouted, "freeze, this is a robbery," he realised he had his back to the counter but the girl handed him a box of cash anyway, you know one of the ones that explodes when you break it open.

So Donny said he was now on the run from all the money lenders in Glasgow, and the cops, and all he had to show for it was this bag of stained red notes and a red face. He was hiding in a pal's flat thinking he has no way out this mess when he sees in the papers that there is a £4000 reward out for him. So he gets his pal to phone the cops and grass him up, and the deal was that his pal got £500 for sticking him in, and the rest would be to pay off all the moneylenders, leaving about £2000 for Donny when he got out. After his time inside (he got four years but got out after about three) he came back to the Argosy and it was as if he was never away. It didn't change him one bit. He would still sit and sing and drink beer and still went to the bookies every day - like I said, every mans has a weakness. Donny passed away with throat cancer; it was sad, he got it cut away and he recovered from it, but then it came

75

back and the doctors told him that this time round he would lose his voice. So Donny didn't tell anyone, he just said no to the op and got on with it. None of the boys knew any of this until after his funeral. Donny Brown, my pal.

If you drink in a pub for long enough you go from listening to stories to telling them and over the years I had a few to tell. The one my dad and the boys liked the most was about our wee pal, Eddie. This wee guy was a diamond of a guy, a pure gentleman. Eddie would come into the pub, always with a bad hangover. One day he came in to tap Gerry, and when Gerry went to the bar to get him a drink the wee guy was choking for a beer that much that he grabbed mine and started to down it before I could stop him. I was like, "Eddie, fucking hell," and he says, "sorry, son, I was choking for a wee sip. I need a drink to sort me out, son". I was OK with it, just laughed it off, because it happens in a pub. Most of them had a drink problem. Now what we couldn't work out was that he told us he drank a bottle of vodka and six cans of beer the night before, but after 2 pints in the pub he was pissed as a fart, but the good thing was that when he was drunk he would sing, and he couldn't sing to save his fucking life. He loved the Beatles so if he sang 'Hey Jude' he would pretend he was playing the piano on the pub table. He would really go for it and all the boys would egg him on, telling him how good he was. One day his wife says to my dad, "are you trying to make a fool of him?" and my dad says, "no, hen, he's doing a good enough job of that himself". When Eddie had had enough drink he would sit down and say, "call me a cab," and we would all shout, "you're a cab !!!"

One night I was walking past his house when I met his daughter who said, "my mum and dad are having a drink. Why don't you go in and say hello?" So I'm thinking 'I could pop in, say "hi" and maybe get a wee drink, so I go in and they are so happy to see me. It was all the "Joe son, sit down," so I sit down to have a few beers and a wee vodka or two, and I'm sitting talking away to wee Eddie and his wife, and to be honest I appreciate it so much bringing me in from the cold and filling me with drink and all the smokes I want – no' bad for a young guy who is skint on a Wednesday night. As the night moved on wee Eddie is up playing the mantlepiece, singing 'Great Balls of Fire' and I'm now being told to help myself to a drink. So I'm in the kitchen going through all the bottles looking to make a strong cocktail and I'm no' giving a fuck how it's going to taste as long as its strong. I found vodka martini and lemonade. I went back into the living room with my shit James bond drink and a can of beer and sat down to have a smoke when I hear Eddie's wife say to the daughter, "right hen, it's time for your dad's bed,". The daughter walks out of the room, then come back in and puts something in Eddie's can of beer - plop! I'm like, "what's going on?" so I ask his daughter and she says, "well, when my dad is drunk and is singing we put a Valium in his beer to get him to sleep, so we can get some peace to watch the TV. I'm like, "fucking hell, how long has this been going on for," and she says, "we've been doing it for years". So when no one was looking I swapped the cans so I could get a good night's sleep. I think I went home around about 11 that night and I was told that wee Eddie stayed up late for the first time in years, singing into the

night. The funny thing about it is for years this poor wee guy
was telling us what he had to drink the night before, and we
were all thinking he was talking shit because after two pints he
was drunk, but he was only drunk because he still had Valium
in his system! The wee guy was more drugged up than a baby
elephant on a BBC wildlife programme.

Do you remember round about the mid-nineties everyone
was selling cheap tobacco and booze? Well, Eddie was doing it.
I never bothered. I didn't smoke roll ups and didn't like cheap
whisky but my dad says to me, "try the dark rum they have -
its good stuff for a fiver". So I went to the pub one Friday and
Eddie only had one bottle of rum and was keeping it for my
dad, but says he would phone his daughter if I wanted to walk
up to his, and pick it up. So I went up there. His kid took her
time to open the door and I'm thinking 'hurry up, you knew I
was coming'. She tells me to go into the back room and get my
rum. The room was like an Aladdin's cave - drink and tobacco
everywhere - so I took three bottles of rum and just walked
out - bye. That night I took a bottle round to my dad and Joe,
and told them what happened and he said, "that's fuck all. I
got my bottle off him and gave him a £20 note. Eddie went
away to get me my change and came back and gave me a £20
and a £5 note". I'm sure you won't be surprised when I tell
you Eddie didn't sell booze and tobacco for long.

There was a lot of things I couldn't get my head around in
the pub but would work it out as I got older - things like all the
caveman stuff and acting the hard man when it came to talking
about birds, even though every guy in the pub was missing a
bird. I caught on really quickly that the pub wasn't the place

you went with girlfriend troubles. I think the only thing they could tell me was to make sure you come first, which was never a problem in my young life. The other unspoken thing was that one or two guys in the pub were gay. No one ever brought it up, especially the gay guys. I mean, no one had a problem with them which was good, but at the same time I had a feeling no one was OK with it, even them, which was crazy. One of them even said to me one night, "Joe, everyone thinks I'm gay. Why is that?" and I said," it's because you are, mate, no big deal". And he went in a wee mood about it and the next day I told my old man what I had said and he went, "you can't say that". I'm like, "why no'. What was the problem with what these guys do in their own time? But again it was how it was in their day, no one talked about it.

In 1999 me and my two pals, Jimmy and Des, had all found ourselves single so we booked a holiday to LA and Vegas - two weeks driving in the sun from LA to Vegas. Half way through our holiday we were in San Diego at the Holiday Inn. We went to the bar that night and got talking to the barman, telling him where we were from and all that shit, so as time went on Jimmy and Des popped out for a smoke and we were drinking Jack and Coke and pints of Bud. So I'm thinking, 'the boys will be back soon. Better get the drinks in'.

I asked the man for the same again and he says, "why?"

I'm like, "what do you mean, why? That's what we're drinking."

And he says, "no, it's the law here that you can only have two drinks at one time, so I can't pour you a beer till that one is done".

79

So I'm thinking 'that's a pretty good thing'. I mean, how many drinks do we waste at nights out in Glasgow at last orders. I finished my beer so I could get another one and the guy says, "where are your friends".

And I say they've both popped out for a wee fag...".

Well, the bar man and a few guys at the end of the bar burst out laughing.

I'm like, "what did I say," and then I work it out- fag in America isn't a cigarette - so I'm, like, "sorry". and the guys at the end of the bar are all cool about it, just still laughing when Jimmy and Des come back. The guys get us a drink saying they want to drink with Scotsmen. We get them to drink whisky and they get us to say a few bad words they can think of.

When we get up in the morning / afternoon I have the hangover from hell. Jimmy and Des hit the pool and I take about an hour just to get a shower, then I head down to the bar for a beer to sort me out. The same barman was on duty and he says he will make me a drink to cure my hangover as long as I don't ask what's in it. So I sit in the shade with my drink looking for my pals but I can't see them. But the guys from last night are down at the pool - two of them, anyway - and one of them is rubbing sun cream on the other's back. Fair enough, but when he lay back after putting the cream on he gave his pal's balls a wee quick rub, too.

I went for another beer and said to the barman, "I didn't realise that two of the guys from last night were gay".

He gives me a surprised look and replies, "of course they're gay. Everyone here is gay. Its gay Pride weekend. "Are you not gay then?" he asks me.

I'm like, "no, I'm just passing through," and he was like, "sure buddy".

As I headed back to the room I met my pals who were now going down to the pool so I'm thinking 'no point in telling them yet. Let them enjoy their day at the pool with the boys,' so I go and get some food, then head back to get a beer at the pool. My pals met me at the bar and they told me how our brand new pals had got us tickets for a day out tomorrow. I told them that unfortunately we were on a deadline to get to Vegas so wouldn't be able to make the day out and I didn't think It would be our thing anyway. We got in the car and I let them in on the secret - that our new pals were gay, and pretty much everyone in town was, too, so let's hit the road. Jimmy was laughing until he remember one of the guys had rubbed sun cream on his back and I'm like, "how did you thank him?" Back home I told the boys in the pub this funny story but they didn't get it, especially my dad. He was like, "maybe you should just go to Spain on holiday..". I'm like, good thinking, Pops, no gay guys in Spain, right?" Good to know some things change for the better in time.

Some guys my age wouldn't even think to sit with the old guys in the pub. They would just see them as some old drunk cunt who talks a load of shit, but they would be wrong. I mean, guys my own age know fuck all, so sitting with someone 'old school,' you always get an interesting or funny story.

One day I was up visiting my wee grandmother and she was talking about her brothers and sisters and I asked her, "where are they all now? " She said most of them had passed away here in Scotland, but a few of them had emigrated to Australia. Her big brother and wee sister moved over there and lived in the same street as each other. She said we didn't like my wee sister's husband - he was a drinker and he would hit her when he was drunk so our big brother made sure he got a house near her to keep an eye on the wee rat. Late One night her brother was in bed when there was a knock on the door. He opened it but at first he thought there was no one there till he looked down and saw his wee sister lying there on his porch, covered in blood. He picked her up, took her inside to his wife and he asked her what had happened. She said her husband had come home drunk and they got into an argument. He punched her a few times and when she got up to leave he grabbed her and pushed her head right through the big fish tank they had in their living room. When she woke up she was lying at her back door and could hear a noise from the back garden so she sat up and saw her husband digging a hole. He must have thought he had killed her so he was getting rid of the body. My gran's sister crawled her way out of the house and over to her big brother's house. She must have been terrified that he was going to notice she was gone before she got there. Her brother went nuts. His wife tried to stop him going over saying, "we can call the police," but he was off. And when he got to the back garden the wee drunk brother-in-law was still digging away with a pickaxe. He was about knee-deep doing a good job for a wee drunk guy. My gran's brother picked up a shovel that was beside the hole and hit the wee fucker right over the head with it. He knocked him out cold and then put him in the hole and sat down at his sister's back door, having a beer and a smoke, waiting on the cops showing up. When the cops did arrive and heard what had happened they let my gran's brother go home and said, "as far as we are concerned you hitting him didn't happen". They just took the wee fucker away to be done with attempted murder and my gran's wee sister never saw him again.

Doesn't Australia sound like a good place to live? I mean, you can beat a guy up and as long as he's a cunt you won't go to prison. Sounds like the place to be. You do that here in Glasgow and you're going to do more time than them. Fuck that! I remember when you got into a fight and the best man won. Now wee neds phone the cops on each other. Back in the day you took a black eye and forgot about it.

Me, my dad and big Shug were sitting having a drink in a pub up north, in the middle of nowhere - it was Glencoe, I think. The pub was just outside the local village, and most of the customers were hill walkers wanting tea and hot soup. We were wanting beer and whisky. The place was run down, the jukebox didn't work, the walls had no paint on them and pictures on the wall were photos of Castlemaine XXXX lager which they had on draft, beer that we hadn't seen in years in Glasgow. But the one thing that the pub had, it's one saving grace apart for alcohol, was it had a big open fire blazing away. I mean, it was a godsend getting out of the cold and sitting by the fire, drinking beer. It was like heaven on earth. Then one of the locals walked in.

"Alright, Hamish. Is that a black eye you have?" the bar man said.

"Yes it is. happened in here last night."

"Who did it?"

"One of the wee lads up from England. Had too much to bloody drink, obviously fancied himself as a fighter."

I walked up to the bar to get a round in and had a look at Hamish. He was over six foot tall and had hands like fucking shovels. I felt like I was in the land of the giants.

As the barman poured my beers he said, "no' like you to take any shit from anyone, Hamish".

"Don't worry about it. I gave them all a bloody good pasting," he replied.

I walked back to our table and told my dad and Shug, "that cunt's hands are as big as fucking shovels," and Shug says "I bet them boys from England are feeling it today".

Everyone in the UK wants to have a fight with a Scotsman because we have a reputation for being hard and everyone from Scotland wants to have a fight with someone from Glasgow because again it is known as a hard city. Fucking hell, it's no' easy being from Glasgow. Only good thing is if you go to America they want to drink with you because again we are known as hard drinkers. I met a few guys in New York one time when I was in a bar there. They were like, "you must have a whisky with us," and me and my pals were like, "sure," so they got out this expensive bottle, started pouring and said, "say when guys". My pals didn't drink whisky so they just had a small one but I stepped up. I'm like, I'm doing this for my country I'm taking one for the team, so I let the guy pour me a double-double, leaving just enough room for some ice and coke. But no one told me we were drinking it straight. Turns out my pals knew and they could tell by the look on my face I fucking didn't, so I took a deep breath and says "for Scotland" and downed it, keeping a straight face.

So back to the hard city of Glasgow. I don't know why we have a bad name because all cities in the UK have bad bits and good bits just like Glasgow. As long as you are known to everyone where you come from, then you get by in life. And people will always say our reputation is because we drink so much, but that's bullshit, too. Scots don't drink strong beers - I mean in Italy they all drink super lager and in Scotland if you drink super lager you're a tramp, but like anything, once you have a bad name it sticks. As I said you only need to shag one sheep to be a sheep shagger.

My dad and his pals would always tell me about growing up in Glasgow and how bad it was. One time my dad was in the town with his cousin who was up to visit from England. They were drinking all day and night in the pubs till closing time and on the way to the train station they went to the chip shop but when they got to the shop most of the shutters were down although the lights were still on. The shutter for the door was still up, though, so my dad banged on the door. A big guy opened it and said, "fuck off," and before my old man could say, "I'm fucking wanting some chips," the door shut in his face. My dad's cousin said, "come on, Arthur, let's go," but my dad, being drunk and hungry, was having none of it. He said to his cousin, I'm going to bang on this fucking door and tell that big cunt I'm no' in the mood to fuck about, now let us in because we know you're still open. Then he said, "get ready," and banged on the door again. It opened and before my old man could have his say the big guy hits my dad on the chin with a knuckle duster - bang - he knocks my dad clean out. Next thing my dad remembers is waking up on the tram tracks. All he remembered was that before the big cunt hit him he had seen a guy standing in the shop with a suit on and he knew his face from somewhere. My dad got up and looked about for his cousin. A few minutes later he could hear a voice calling for him, "Arthur! Arthur!"

My dad found him down an alleyway; the poor guy was in some mess and my old man knew it was all his fault. My dad picked him up and asked if he needed to go to the hospital. His cousin said, "no, just get me home". The poor guy - he tried to explain to the guys in the shop he had nothing to do with it but they didn't listen.

My old man asked him what happened?

He said, "after they knocked you clean out three guys walked out the shop; one of them was the main man and he told the other two to drag you onto the tram line, then they dragged me round the back. I tried to explain that we were just wanting chips and the guy in the suit says,

"you tell your fucking pal the next time he gets in my way I'll put him in front of a train instead of a tram, OK?" My old man got him home and poured him a drink.

Then his cousin said, "Arthur, who is Jimmy Boyle?"

My old man's blood ran cold. "Why you asking that," my dad asked.

"Well the guy who owned the shop ran past me after the guys walked away and says are you OK, son? I said yes, and he said you're pal took a chance there, messing with Jimmy Boyle. He was in me shop getting his protection money". I told the guy we didn't know, and he said get yourself home and ran into the night.

When my dad told me that story I said, "I've never met that cousin".

H said, "take a wild guess why".

I loved sitting in the pub hearing everyone's stories because as long as a guy has a drink beside him anything goes when they are telling a tale. Sometimes they're happy tales and some are sad, but the funniest ones were the dirty ones. Like when one of the guys in the pub was abroad with his family and he went into a shop for a pair of sunglasses. When he got back to the beach with his new specs his daughter asked him if his new specs were for women?

He said, "no, hen," and she said

"are you sure? They look like women's sunglasses".

He said the guy in the shop told me they are anal sex glasses. Well, his stunned family didn't know what to say till his daughter went,

"don't you mean unisex, dad?" and he said

"same thing, hen," trying to talk his way out of it.

I was telling a few of the boys about the time my ex-girlfriend had an Ann Summers party in our flat. The deal back then was that if you are the host of the party you get a free gift. So I went to the pub and left her and her pals to get pissed and tell dirty stories.

The next morning I asked, "how did it go?"

She said the girl who worked for Ann summers was great fun and she had them doing drinking games and all checking out the handcuffs and whips and then as the night went on and everyone had a good few drinks in them the girl said,

"it's time to find out a few dark secrets from you girls. Come on. Everyone has a wee secret.

Now I knew most of the girls at the party so I was wanting to know who said what. One of the girls was, well, a big girl - I mean, I don't want to say she was fat but she was no stranger to a fish supper. Anyway, as the night was in full swing the girls were looking through the Ann Summers book and this girl kept saying at every page I have that, or I have those; I mean, she had everything in the fucking book, even, my girlfriend told me in confidence, the edible pants. Well fuck me, I almost fell out of the bed: fucking edible pants - how big were these things. You would have needed a cup of tea to wash them down the size she was, well apart from the bits that were all soggy from her body sweat...sorry, too far! Well, then the girls were all having a drink and swapping stories, like how they got really drunk at the Christmas party and kissed some married guy, and all that bullshit, but when it came round to the big girl's turn to tell a secret, she said ,

"I don't have any secrets," and the girls are thinking 'shit, she probably hasn't had many boyfriends or anything'. But they keep at her, giving it all that "are you sure" until she says,

"well I do have one," and they all cheer and shout, "tell us! tell us!"

She says, "a few years ago I worked at Ibrox in the canteen and my boss was married but he liked me and said it wasn't working out with him and his wife".

So all the girls are like, "oh, did you kiss him?"

And she said, "yeah, after my shift was done and everyone

went home he would take me up to the pool room, make me take my clothes off and get me to sit naked on the pool table. Then he hit the pool balls as hard as he could off my fanny and asked me if I liked it".

The room was dead silent. Well, it was silent the next day when I was being told the story. I was sure I was going to pass out with laughing. I kept thinking at the time players like Paul Gascoigne and Ally McCoist, who were at Rangers at this time, must have been playing pool then having a beer and trying to work out why their fingers were smelling of fish. I couldn't get over it and my girlfriend kept saying it was sad, not funny, and asked me not to tell anyone. Well, that lasted about three hours until I went to the pub and met my old man. How could I keep that from the boys - come on!

A few weeks later I got a slip through my door saying I had missed the postman so because I was working all week I asked my old man to go to the post office and pick it up for me. The next day after work I went up to his to get it.

"It's a big box," he said, "what did you order?" and I couldn't think of anything till I opened it and the first thing I pulled out was a whip and then a big vibrator.

My poor old dad's face! He was like, "what the fuck?"

I said, "this is the Ann Summers stuff from the party a few weeks ago".

He took one look and said, "if I was walking about the streets with that and the cops stopped me, they would have put me away thinking I was an old pervert". Then he was like, "look at the size of that thing! Women don't need men anymore, not when they have a toy cock the size of a fucking truncheon".

I told him, "it's a new world, dad. Girls just want an orgasm or two, and you're right - they don't need an old fucker like you".

Then my old man, sharp as ever said, "yeah, well I might be too old to stir the gravy but I can still lick the spoon".

Question - have you ever been in a fight in a pub? Anyone who has will tell you it's no' like the movies where two guys fight it out with their fists for about ten minutes. No, it's fuck all like that. It's always two or more guys who will do anything to win, which means they look like a couple of stupid cunts punching and kicking each other, covered in beer and blood, falling about drunk. I've been in a few fights but no' that many over the last thirty years, thank fuck, because it's a nightmare when you just want a good day or night out, and someone is being a pain in the ass. The only good thing is I didn't get hurt, or hurt anyone else in any of them; the only thing I hurt any guy with was his pride, but that heals. Most of the time you don't need to fight. You can shut the argument down with a straight face and a few hard words. And the rules you stick with - like I never did all that outside bullshit. No. If some cunt is saying they want to take you outside to kick the shit out of you, why wait? I would just hit the fucker there and then. I never waited for anyone to hit first. Even in school I always told my kids, there is no waiting. If someone says, "I'll get you after school," then just hit them there and then. Show them you are no' fucking about. Gets them off guard every time.

The only thing with a pub fight is there are pint glasses everywhere and that is when someone can really get hurt. I've

seen a guy pull John Bone's chair away from him. John was
holding the old glass pint with a handle on it. He didn't spill
a drop of his beer but got up as fast as he went down and
hit the guy, who was standing laughing at him, right over the
head with his glass. The guy hit the floor faster than a cow's
knickers. And a guy did the same to my old man; he didn't
have a pint, but he had a cigarette in his hand,. He got up and
put the cigarette out on the guy's nose. The guy was walking
about like it was Comic Relief for weeks. A few times I hit
people with a glass but it was in anger, I would just throw it
at them. I never tried to use it as a weapon. One time I only
threw it at the guy because I had stuck the head in him, and he
was a big fucker and was walking back towards me for more. I
was like, shit, so I hit him with a pint just to put the wind up
him and it worked. He got off out the door, and I got dragged
out the back door and told never to return.

I could always see a fight was coming in the pub. It's
weird. You can feel it in the air or you see tell-tale signs like
some guy getting loud and then he goes to the bar and buys a
bottle of beer when he has been drinking pints all day. The one
thing my old man always told me was don't get involved - the
guy who tries to split up the fight is the one who always gets
a sore face so let them get on with it. They're adults anyway,
so fuck them. Years ago my mum had a boyfriend and he was
going to the Argosy for a drink and was always saying "hello"
or waving over to me, so I got a hold of him out of the way
and said, "look I don't know you in this pub. If my old man
finds out you're my mum's boyfriend he'll go nuts," and he
was like, "OK, sorry," but a few days later he would be at it

again - waving and looking over at me. It was pissing me off so I told my mum to have a word with him. She said he's only trying to be your pal, and I was like, I don't need another pal. So one Sunday me and my old man are sitting having a few beers. I was on the Guinness as I like it in the winter - can't drink it in the summer, it's like a bowl of soup. Anyway, me and my dad are talking shit when he said, "who's that guy over there". I look over and it's my mum's boyfriend again. I said I don't know who it is and my dad is like, "he's been coming in for a while now and keeps looking over here".

I'm like, "no, you're stoned," and just then this tit sits about two tables away and says

"Hi Joe, how are you?"

I saw red! I shouted, "see you cunt, you must be really fucking stupid or really smart, trying to fuck with my head".

He said, "I don't know what I've done, Joe," so I hit him with my pint.

It exploded all over him and everyone at the next table.

He ran to the bar and said, "he hit me, bar him".

The barmaid said, "I've known Joe a long time and for him to do that you must have done something to make him do it, so you're barred. And don't come back".

And that's why I love drinking in the Argosy.

The old saying never judge a book by its cover is so true when you drink in a pub like the Argosy. I mean, guys from all these different walks of life - guys who had done time or were dealing drugs, and they didn't look like criminals. Most of the nutters just look like the guy next door. That's why in Glasgow you need to watch who you're talking to in a pub, because he could be a postman or a fucking nutcase - they all dress the same. And it goes the other way, too. Some guys look really bad-ass but could turn out to be the nicest guys you could ever meet. I remember a good few years ago, the Argosy had a singer on a Saturday night - Jane someone. I can't remember her second name but all the old guys in the pub loved her from back in the sixties. She was tipped to be just as big as Lulu, but missed out. Anyway she was in the pub singing one Saturday night, and her boyfriend was this quiet guy with a ponytail and sunbed tan. He didn't say anything; he just set up for her then walked about the pub watching her sing on stage. So me and another friend, Wullie (I'll tell you about how I met him a bit later on) were talking about him having a ponytail, and my old man said, "watch what you say. He might be a nutter; you never know". Within a week or two word went round the camp fire that he was a right hard case, there to lookout for this bird, make sure no one fucked with her. Then people would say, yeah, he did some hard time, and this and that. But it was all hearsay. No one knew who or what he was. Then one Saturday night he walked up to the back of the lounge where just me and Wullie were sitting and I'm thinking, shit, he's going to dig us, and my old man and his pals aren't here. So the guy walks up to our table. Me and Wullie are stoned and paranoid at the best of times, but now we're like two deer caught in the head lights. It felt like he'd been standing over us for hours when I said, "alright," and in the most polite voice he said, "any chance yous boys could get me a wee bit of hash". He was too polite! I almost burst out laughing but we were like, "sure mate," and he was all, "thanks very much. I'll

93

give you a bit for a few joints, guys," which was music to our skint ears. All the old gossip was done. The so called hard man was, in fact, brand new.

All we had to do was talk to the guy to find out, but even some of the guys you did talk to you were still no' sure about. I mean for a start they drank in the Argosy which had always had a bad name. There was a guy who came in to tap money off Gerry for years. He had long white hair like Billy Connolly and a big scar from his ear to his chin, and it was deep into the bone. I mean, you couldn't miss it and I could never take my eyes off it. I kept wondering how he got it. Maybe a bar fight or a drug deal gone wrong, For years I would try and work out how, but I never asked. Then one day he came in for a tap and an old drunk guy at the next table says, "hey mate, how did you get that Mars bar on your face?" I said, "hey nose out, old yin," but the guy says, "no it's OK. I was in the army and was doing a parachute jump one night, and when I landed I noticed I was stuck in the dark and couldn't move. Turned out I'd landed on a barbwire fence and I didn't know it had slashed my face until I noticed one side of my face was warm from the blood". I was sitting thinking, "fuck me, all these years and I would never have worked that one out. After that, it turned out he was a sound guy and really funny, too.

As the years went on he would stay for a drink and a joint and talk shit like the rest of us, and he would hit out with random stuff like, "why do junkies get free drugs, and us alcoholics get fuck all?" and that's the best way to start a debate in a pub. Just put it out there. Because I was in on what he said I was, like, "yeah, I work pay tax and get fuck all, no' even a biscuit. These cunts don't work and get free drugs". Then my old man said, "if the government was to give you a free packet of biscuits what would you pick?" So then it went from spending our tax money on junkies to our favourite biscuits. One guy would say "chocolate digestive," and everyone would say "good choice". No one would say, "let's get back to what's happening to our hard earned tax money". No. that moment had passed. We are talking biscuits because everyone is stoned and thinking about getting home to a mug of tea and a packet of Jaffa Cakes.

DIGGING UP
THE PAST WILL
JUST GET YOU
DIRTY.

CHAPTER 4

Too Skint to O.D

When I moved to Penilee in 1990 I was a lost soul. Like any 15 year old kid I missed my pals in Pollok. It felt like I was all alone for years, but looking back now it was only a month or two and then I met Chris Fla and the rest of the boys down the line. First it was me and Fla and his pal, Mark Reid. His dad drank in the pub with my old man. Me and Mark hit it off; we both like music and getting stoned. Then Fla's cousin, Brian Law, Big Law's nephew, started popping round. Brian was the life and soul, he was always messing about making everyone laugh and he was up for getting stoned, too. Only thing with Brian was he wasn't a drinker. His mum always said two cans and he has the hiccups, and she was right. But Brian still loved to get drunk. Mark Reid didn't drink. He was all about the hash which was cool with us, but after a few weeks of getting stoned I was wanting a beer one weekend. Fla and Mark were looking at that as the more beer we buy, the less hash we can get, so I was like, "OK, I'll go," and Fla was like, no, you're right mate. Let's get the beers in". A few weekends Mark wouldn't show up, and as time went on that happened more and more. and Fla was taking it personally. I was like, "let the guy do what he wants, we're all still pals," but Fla loved being in a gang. I mean, it was OK just me and him on the odd night, but he loved all the guys in one room, taking the piss out of each other. There was nothing he loved more than sitting with the boys. As time went on Brian told us he had a pal, Wullie, who stayed two doors down from him and he was just like us; he loved music and he liked getting drunk. He kept on saying you need to meet him, so one night Brian said that Wullie was baby-sitting his two wee nephews round the corner and that we should pop in, so we did. Wullie was just like us, ripped jeans, Pink Floyd tee shirt, he even had curly hair like me that we both hated having. So Brian took us in and introduced us and that's how I met Wullie.

It was about midnight and Wullie is like, "come in and get a seat. Do you want a drink?"

And we are like, "sure".

He opens his aunt's drinks cabinet and says, "what would you like?"

"Are you sure this is OK?"

"Yeah," he says, "if we all agree to have just two bottles between us my aunt won't notice," so we opened a bottle of vodka and a bottle of rum.

That night we all got on so well, and I remember thinking that this could turn out to be a cool gang of pals. We sat about talking and playing music. Wullie was a drummer in a band from Govan where he grew up and I liked that he was like me, he didn't grow up in the Pen either, so we had that in common. He told us we could hang here every weekend if we wanted and we were like, "hell, yes!" An empty house every fucking weekend. How cool was that. Think of all the birds we could invite. Well, to be honest, we could invite loads but none would fucking show up. Wullie had a girlfriend, Roseann, and he was nuts about her, but her mum kept her away from him and that fucked Wullie up over the years.

Anyway back to the night we met; we sat talking, drinking, playing his music collection, and Wullie asked us if we liked Supertramp. I said I didn't know who they were. He gave me their album, 'Crime of the Century'. He was like, "take this and listen to it. You'll love it," and he was right, because thirty years later and I still listen to it. Looking back now I can still remember all of that night. I've forgotten a lot of things over the years, maybe because of too much drink or drugs, but that night I can still see us all sitting in that house like I'm a fly on the wall. Maybe I remember it because it was the beginning of an amazing journey of friendship and being a teenager, I don't know, but it was the night where it all began for us four young boys. If we only knew what lay ahead in the next 30 years of high and dry, happy and sad, good times and bad times.

Looking back now we were just lost souls kicking about the streets of Penilee, rain or shine we would be out, money or no money we would just walk about looking to see what we would find round the next corner, and most of the time we didn't find anything good - just other young guys with nothing to do, so you knew they would give you a "hi, alright mate" or a "what the fuck you looking at" and we would be in, because you could never run. If you ran away, your pals would never forgive you for that. I mean you could fuck your pal's bird and he would get over it in time but running away from a fight was the end of your membership in the gang. And I'm sad to say it happened to us.

One cold dark night me, Chris, Wullie, Brian and one of Wullie's pals, a guy called Kenny, were walking about the streets at, like, two in the morning. We were heading to cut through the keyhole which takes you onto the Farm Road. We walked past a couple getting out of a taxi after a night out and the guy just stood looking at us. I knew this cunt was drunk and looking for a fight. We were all then aged between 16 and 18 and he was in his late 20s, but to him he was thinking 'I can take all of them on and look like a hard man in front of my bird'. As we walked past him, only me and Kenny saw him looking at us, and Kenny being a young fucking daft kid says to him, "do you want to propose?" That gave the guy all he needed to go ahead with us. He must have had a bat by his front door because within a second he went for us. Kenny shouted, "run!!!" And him and Brian were off. You didn't need to tell Brian twice to run he would always go on the first shout. Me and Wullie went next and Chris was still standing trying to work out what was happening when the guy hit him in the legs with the bat. Wullie looked back, saw what was happening and said to me Joe, "we need to go back," and as we headed back we saw the guy get a knife off his girlfriend standing at her gate. I couldn't work out why a woman would go into her home and get her drunk boyfriend a knife to set about five young kids. So as me and Wullie got back we saw him take the knife and head over to Chris, who was on the ground.

I shouted, "you fucking cunt, he has four brothers who'll come after you for this,"

and the guy says to Chris as he's getting up, "what's your

name?"

"Chris Fla" he say but the guy still looked like he was going to stab him, so I shouted, "you fucking touch him and your fucking cow of a girlfriend will get stabbed, you fucking fat cunt".

He looked up at me and ran for me and Wullie. We were like, "shit, move," so the two of us took off with this nutter with a knife at our backs. As we were running I looked back and saw he was right behind us and keeping up. That's when your head starts to think, 'this shit just got real, if I don't keep running I could be getting stabbed to death'. We got to the end of the street and could only go straight ahead to Linburn Road, or take a right onto Honeybog Road. I went straight on and Wullie went right. I'm no' going to lie when I tell you I have never been more relieved when that mad fucking nutter took a right after Wullie . I ran up to the lane in Linburn and peeked out of it onto Honeybog and couldn't see anyone. That's the shit bit ,when it all goes quiet and you don't know where your pals are, or if they are OK. Chris lived in Honeybog at that time, so I just waited. After about 10 minutes Wullie was hiding in a garden and could see the mad cunt walking up and down the street, then he just went back to where his girlfriend lived. We all showed up then. Then it was the blame game as we were all shouting at each other. Wullie asked who ran first and Brian said it was me.

I lost it with him, but then looked at Chris and Wullie and I said, "do you think it was me, too?"

They both said, "we don't know, it all happened so fast," and I was like, "fuck you,". I came back with, "where the fuck was the other two the whole time? Know what? Fuck this. I have work in the morning unlike you cunts. I'm off," and that was the last night for that young gang.

I went to my work and for a few weeks got drunk in the pub with my old man and his pals. We all still hung about as pals but it all changed that night. Kenny was never seen after that and we were OK with that. Brian, I think introduced Chris to two brothers that he and I knew from school, Scott and Stuart who became real good pals and are still my pals to this day. Wullie went away and got lost in Govan, which he did a lot when he wanted to get out the way from some dealer he owed money to. The days ahead after that were better times with good pals, but I always knew Chris never got over that night. I think he liked having a wee gang to be in, or maybe he was just one of those guys who can't help looking back.

When you think back about your childhood and all your friends there is always one moment in time you remember, like a holiday abroad or a stag party. But with my old pals we didn't have any of that; we lived too fast and most of us lost touch over the years. I mean, by the time we were all about eighteen or nineteen we were staying with our girlfriends and some of us were already parents, and then into our twenties and thirties life had taken all of us down different roads. The only one time I remember us all being together was when Brian's mum and dad went away to Greece for three weeks and left him alone in the house. Fuck knows what they were thinking but we had a ball. Everyone came and went, night and day; it was just a three week nonstop party: drink, hash, acid, whatever. We could buy or tap and we got it within

about five days. We ran out of food but we still only spent
what money we had on drink and drugs. The only way we
got food was for me, Wullie, Scott or Fla to bring some back
from our mums' houses. We watched the film 'The Doors' all
day long, stoned, then at night got drunk and played the tunes.
Brian's two next door neighbours never phoned the cops on
us - God knows they should have because we were going nuts
some nights. It would be just a few of the boys sometimes and
other nights everyone from the scheme was in and as the days
went on people would go and not come back, maybe thinking
'that's it for me, time to get back to work' but a few of us
stayed till the end. It didn't matter how hungry you got or how
much you wanted a hot bath, we didn't go because we didn't
want to miss a thing.

Girls came and went. After one night they'd see it was all
madness and even one night was too much for some of them.
I remember a few girls walking in one night and one of them
caught my eye straight away. I went over and said "hi" and
she said she liked my Stones T-shirt but it seemed that's all
she liked. Fla and Scott sat talking to them because they knew
them but didn't go out of their way to help me out in putting
a good word in for me. I tried hanging about beside them but
I was hovering about like a helicopter in trouble and within an
hour or two the girls left. But not to worry; about a year later
I got to know that girl and we were together for about five
years. So back to the party - me, Brian and Wullie were the last
men standing. We had lost track of time and reality. One night,
about four in the morning, we were on acid dancing about the
living room like you do on a Wednesday at 4 am. We danced

out the front door and started to look at the stars. we thought they were amazing. We had our hands up in the air like we were asking God to save us and as we were walking around the garden I saw a neighbour, an old woman, watching us. I suddenly thought 'what the fuck are we doing?' I was like, "right boys, time to go in now. Let's go." The poor old dear must have thought we were nuts.

One of Brian's sisters popped in to check on us from time to time but Angie was just as bad as us at that time in her life and sometimes she would just stay and party with us. Me and Angie had a bit of a past, so some nights we would sit up late talking. Shit, the boys would give Brian a hard time about it, but the one good thing was that whenever Angie showed up she would have a bag full of drugs so the boys would always send me up to her room. "Go on mate, make us proud." But the truth was that by then me and Angie were just mates who sat up late talking, and maybe kissing. But her room was good for me it got me away from the madhouse for a wee bit.

By the time Brian's mum and dad got back the house was wrecked. They went fucking mad and were right to do so. We all went on the run and after a few days I was the only one out of everyone that went to face the music; only me and Brian took it on the chin. Brian got the shit kicked out of him and I was told that me and the rest of the guys would have to pay them £25 each for the damages, so I went to Wullie, Fla, Scott and Stuart and told them. But they all told me, "yeah, sure thing mate, fuck that!" so I went and saw Brian's mum, and she said if you pay and you get any of them to pay I will give you your money back. So I got Wullie and said that if we paid

£50 we'd get £25 of it back and it makes it all go away, so we sent round the £50 but we never did get the £25 back which I always found funny. Brian's mum got us back, and to be fair £25 is no' bad for three weeks rent is it?... three weeks party. We didn't know if it was New York or New Year and these days I couldn't party for three hours, never mind three weeks.

Wullie didn't know when to stop. He would be on it for days on end. Maybe it was to keep the demons at bay or maybe he just liked to get fucked up, but what we know now that we didn't know then was that booze and drugs just feed your demons. It's like trying to run from the devil. He will never overtake you, but he will always be right behind you on your back and that was Wullie's life. He was too young to find a way out. We would meet up and get on it and two days later I would stop and go back to work, then go and find him five days later still on it, sitting with guys and girls taking shit drugs and drinking cheap drink, and he had only just met them. So I would be like, "OK, time to go home". He would be so burnt out he would let me take him home. We all did it from time to time but Wullie knew how to party hard. With the drink it was OK because you would drink so much or too much, then be sick and go home but with drugs you would last for days thinking you were fine. We got into theses pills called 'speed bombs'. Fuck knows what was in them but they would keep you going for days, never up or down. Fla called them truck driver's pills because they kept you going throughout the night.

Every now and then we would go somewhere else for a pint away from the Argosy, maybe try and get a bird, but it was always a nightmare. We were 18 years old and girls at that age wanted a guy with a car, no' a guy with a drink and drug habit. One night we walked into a working mans' club and the bingo was on. This place was full of drunk females. "OK, this is the night, Wullie. Let's no' fuck it up. So we got talking to two young girls. They seemed to be just as drunk as us and up for a good time. The night was going great. They asked us back to a flat one of them had, so we were well happy. I'm ready for a wee party. Just before the club shut I went for a piss and found out when I got back to the table that Wullie had jumped a taxi with one of the birds and left me with the other one and her mum. Yeah! that's right- her fucking mum. Turns out her mum had been sitting at the next table the whole time and was now wanting a lift back home in the taxi. I was hovering about like a helicopter in trouble trying to work out how the fuck I was getting out of this. The girl says, "it'll be fine. We'll drop my mum off, then go to my pal's flat". I was still no' sure, sitting drinking my beer, over-thinking the situation like I was Ethan Hunt, but what really was on my mind was the Ethan Hunt who had fucked off and left me with the fucking Waltons.

The taxi journey got a bit uncomfortable. Her mum was in the front and I'm trying to make small talk with her, when the daughter puts her jacket over my lap, smiles, winks at me, then grabs my dick. I'm thinking 'what the fuck,' maybe we should drop your mum off first I gave her a look like, 'not just now' but it didn't work. She was pulling on me like she was unblocking a fucking sink. I'm trying to play it cool, still talking away to her mum, saying stuff like, "so do you and your palsssss go out every weekendddd !!." The poor woman didn't have a clue, thank fuck. so we dropped the old dear off, then went to dig up my pal at the flat. But when I showed up Usain Bolt was already in the room going for it. I'm thinking you'll keep till the morning, pal. Me and the other girl went into the living room for a drink.

I asked, "does your pal have a dog?"

"No, why?" she asked.

I said, "just asking".

She asked me what I did for a living I told her I'd just been thrown out of the SAS for being a bully.

She went "really?"

I'm like, "yeah, sure, where's the bedroom?" and about two hours later after I had disappointed the poor girl a few times I got up to have a drink with Wullie, who was waiting on me with our carry-out in his hand.

"Let's go," he said, and I'm like, "OK, but what's the hurry?" as he pushed me out the door.

Turns out once Wullie had sobered up he didn't think much of his bird.

"She had big fucking buck teeth," he said, and I said they were no' that bad but he went, "she could eat an apple through a letterbox".

I was like, "yeah, mine wasn't any better. I think she's dropped more boxers than Mike Tyson. She was all over my dick like it was a fucking ice cream cone on a hot day. I swear I had to hold on to the headboard she was riding me like Sea Biscuit".

There was always a lot of people coming and going from Scott and Stuart's house but the four main usual suspects was me, Chris, Scott and Stuart. Everyone else would show up from time to time. The four of us all had this mad routine that we would sit with each other; like I could sit with just Scott, smoke a joint, have a beer and talk shit, and we could sit there all night like two good pals. It was the same with Chris or Stuart, but if the four of us were sitting together we could never see eye to eye. It was mad. I don't know what it was. I knew Scott and Stuart, being brothers, they would never get on, but the four of us were really good pals. But maybe that's just the way young guys are. Me and Scott would spend a lot of time together while Chris was kissing his bird at her front door. We would sit and smoke his dope and play his music. You could hear him running back up the street because he knew we had his hash. Stuart and me spent a lot of time together back then because our girlfriends were pals. Brian and Stuart went to school together and were good pals for years and Brian didn't like how me and Stuart were getting along again. I don't know why, but Brian was coming and going back then; he was doing a lot of drugs, a lot of bad shit and he knew we would dig him for it so he would hide it from us.

One night me and Stuart were chilling when he went out for about ten minutes, then came back in with a matchbox full of hash and gave it to me to roll a joint.

I said, "where did you get this."

He said, "don't worry about it," so I didn't.

I was well happy with a bit of free hash but a few nights later he did the same thing again and I was like, "what's going on? Who's hash is this? "

Again he said, "don't worry about it," but the next day I

said, "I know it's only a shit bit of hash, but it's someone's hash ,and I don't want any more."

So Stuart went, "OK, keep this to yourself. There's a family in this street that I know, and the mom is watching all the drugs for this scheme in her house behind her fire place. She's out at work, but her son is home. Come on, and I'll show you," so we went into the house.

The son was so stoned I think he didn't know if it was New York or New Year. They pulled out a bag from behind the fire place and it was full blocks of hash, acid strips, bags of speed and pills.

I told them, "I don't think you should be showing anyone that, no' even me."

So they are like, "no one knows about it," and I'm like, "good, keep it that way," and we walked out the house and never went back.

A few weeks went past and I didn't say a thing about it. I knew most of the drug dealers and I knew they didn't fuck about. They were OK with me because I paid up front for my hash, and didn't tic them like some of my pals, then avoid them for weeks on end.

Two or three weeks had passed and I went round to see Chris, and he said "do you know the house bla bla…and all the rest", and I was like "yeah, I think so," and he said, "well they've been minding the drugs and some cunt has gone in and took the lot, and Scott thinks it might have been Stuart and Brian".

So I told Chris I had seen it, but didn't want anything to do with it. As soon as I'd seen it I was off out the house and didn't talk about it to anyone. I went to see Stuart. I knew just from looking at him he didn't do it and I asked him if Brian knew about it because I knew it was the sort of thing that Brian would do. But he said Brian hadn't known about it. Turned out it was a guy called Mackay; he went to school with me and Scott he was an OK guy but I didn't get on with him, although Scott did. Anyway Mackay knew the family, too. Found out what was going on and broke in and took the lot. I couldn't believe it was him because he didn't take a lot of drugs but it turned out he was just getting into them and hit them hard. He was seen running about Govan with this bag trying to make pals, but he never did. The guys in Govan helped him take all the drugs, then told him to fuck off. His family lived in the same street the drugs were taken from, and got a visit from two guys who told them they had to pay a few grand, or Mackay was no more; and even after the debt was paid Mackay was to stay away from the scheme. We heard later that the family, I think his poor wee mum, had to sell her house to pay it off, but that was just the word round the campfire at the time. One thing I do know is Mackay didn't get over it. He was in deep with the drugs and died a young guy, only in his thirties, maybe. That happens a lot with guys who start later on in life taking drugs. Fla would call them 'late to the party guys' and he was right. They seemed to be on catch-up; they would go full throttle then bang, game over.

Every night was party night. Everyone would show up to get stoned and play music. We all had our favourite bands: mine was, and still is, The Rolling Stones, for Chris, The Who, Scott, Pink Floyd, Stuart was into rap which we never let him play and Brian was The Beatles. Me and Brian would sit in a corner for hours debating on who was the best band - The Stones or the Beatles. I mean, we would go over it for hours and hours. All the other guys were chatting up the girls while I was telling Brian that 'Gimme Shelter' was the best rock 'n' roll song ever. and it is, by the way. We would go over songs albums and best singers like two guys fighting over Celtic and Rangers. That was the one good thing about back then, none of us were into football. They will tell you that's bull-shit but I don't ever remember us all sitting down to watch a game. We were 100% music fans and maybe the boys were too stoned to know the game was on.

I always liked it when it was just a few of us. Like I said, when we all sat in the same room it didn't always go well. One summer's night Wullie showed up with his girlfriend, Roseann, who me and Scott knew from school. Wullie was madly in love with Roseann. They had a young child and were living together so we didn't see much of Wullie at that time, which wasn't a bad thing because as much as me and Chris were good pals with him, we knew he was a wild card, and could kick off at any time. And guess what happened that summer's night? Yeah. He went for it. We were all sitting talking and carrying on, everyone smoking and drinking and I'm watching Wullie having the time of his life, then Wullie didn't like something Brian had said and I'm like, here we go. Roseann knew, too. She was like, "it's time to go," but Wullie stood up to fight. Brian and Stuart told him to take it outside which made him go off big time. Our mate, Rolly, got pushed back by Wullie and cut his hand on a glass and then he went nuts. So me, Chris, Scott and Stuart had to get the two of them out the door, and we all fell onto the street. Roseann got stuck into Wullie about how he was acting, and then walks away.

Wullie turns to me and said, "let's go and get high".

I'm like, "no mate, go get your bird".

He says, "fuck her. I have money. Now let's go".

Roseann hears what he is saying and turns back. There was about twelve of us standing in the street and someone said "she's walking back", so Wullie plays it cool and sits up on an electric box. She walks through us all, gets to Wullie and starts kissing him, and I mean kissing like you see in the movies. She runs her hands down his body, grabs his feet and flips him backwards off the box. He lands head first on the ground, she takes the money out his hand and walks away into the night, not looking back. The twelve of us standing about are speechless. Then someone says, "that's the coolest thing I've ever seen". About two minutes later Wullie woke up and ran after her which we were OK with.

That was the way he led his life. Wullie had demons from a young age. He was a troubled soul. Every night out it would kick off, but it was only because he wouldn't take shit from anyone. You know when you're at a night out, and someone says something trying to be funny at your expense and you think, 'fuck it, I'll let it pass because it's so and so's party'. I don't want to fuck up their night because of this dick-head thinking he's a funny cunt'. No, not Wullie. He wouldn't think twice. He would just go for them and most of the time they asked for it, but it was always my poor pal who got the blame for no' taking any shit. I lost count of how many parties we were told to leave early and even if he was in the wrong I would always go with him because he was my mate. We knew the meaning of the word pals so one minute you're at a party trying to chat up some bird and the next minute your pal is out the front fighting her dad and then you're giving your cans back and told to do one. Don't know how many nights it would end up with just me and Wullie sitting in my room drinking and smoking; just two young pals feeling the whole world was against us. But like all my pals we would stick by each other. If one of us was to go, then we all went. We all had each other's backs. We all came from broken homes. We were a gang, but not like a gang going out looking for trouble. We were just a gang of lads who were all going through the same shit in life, so we went through it together.

I've always said if we had money back when we were young then we would have never made it past 21, and that's a fact. We never had any money so we had to get it from our mums, or we had to steal it from somewhere, anywhere, as long as we got a few bucks for a smoke and a few cans of beer. As soon as we got an £8 bit of hash and six cans of beer life was good. It's the simple things in life! We had drugs, drink and music. What more could a young guy ask for? Well, his hole a guess but we couldn't get a bird in a pet shop, you know. No' having a car or any good gear means you had no chance with the ladies so we had to make do with what we had.

Me, Fla, Brian and Wullie never really dealt drugs but we did get mixed up in some one night. Me and Brian got paid £200 to drop off a bag of smack and get the money for it in

Castlemilk. Now I would say that Castlemilk is a cunt of a place and it is, but anywhere in Glasgow is a cunt of a place if you don't know it, and they don't know you. So we got a taxi. Yes, that right. A fucking taxi, because if the cops stop you, you can put it under the driver's seat and say to the cops that's no' mine. When we got to the address it was high-rise flats so up the lift we go to this door. When we knocked on it the guy told us two minutes; he had to unlock all the locks on the fucking thing. We walked in to the flat and it was like a palace. I mean, it was mint. Big fireplace, big TV, the lot. The guy we met, I was told on the taxi ride up, was the boss of all the door men in Glasgow. He was sitting with no top on, a few tattoos back in the days when people didn't have a lot of tattoos, and he was wearing more gold then MR T. The guy was talking to Brian and he was drinking vodka out of the bottle, and was asking if we would like some. To tell you the truth I was needing some because I was shitting it.

As they were talking I was just looking around and he says, "what you thinking about kid?"

I said, "nothing mate".

He went, "no, tell me".

So I went, "this flat is the best looking flat I've ever seen".

And he went, "is there a but?"

"Yeah" I said. "If you have so much money why don't you buy a bungalow or a back and front door?"

And he says, "because if the cops kick your door in and you stay in a bungalow where can you throw your stash? Up here I can throw it right onto the railway line".

After that Brian got the money and the guy phoned us a

taxi and told us to wait outside the flats for it. As we standing at the door of the flats I heard this noise shooting past my ear. I looked down and stuck in the grass was a wallpaper scraper. I looked up and there was a guy hanging out the window about twenty floors up. The cunt had just missed my head with a fucking wallpaper scraper. I was like, "where is this fucking taxi". Never again.

A few times me and Brian moved that smack about and Brian would skim some off the top. We would sell it on, and fuck me, we made a few bucks. We had new clothes, big bit of hash in our pockets and we could drink in the pub every night. This all lasted for about three weeks but looking back it was like a life time. The only bad thing was we decided to smoke some smack to see what the big deal was. So we rolled it in our joints with hash in it, too. One night we were in the pub and my dad and a few of the boys were really drunk, and one of them dug me about no' passing the joint. I looked at Brian and went, "fuck it." Just then Fla walked in, got a seat beside us and his eyes lit up when he saw me pulling a big ass joint out of my pocket.

He was like, "I'm next on that bad boy".

When I passed it he was taking big long drags of it and saying it smelt funny. Me and Brian are like, "hey, take your time".

My dad and his pals were all stoned - I mean, really gone. Then Fla heads to the bar to get the drinks in. He kept looking back, trying to remember the round and I knew I had to help him. I was like, "right Smokey Joe, get a seat. I'll get this".

We told him about two days later and he was like, "you

bastards! Have you got any more?"

And unfortunately we did. We had loads of it and it was free so what you going to do? Get stoned for free or pay for hash to get stoned? We went for the first option and for about three weeks we all smoked it in joints, and all I remember is nothing. We were so stoned and full of Guinness it was all a blur and I'm sorry to any wee wife's husband that we got stoned on that shit, when he was only out for a pint thinking he was getting a few puffs of hash in the pub on his day off work.

The whole smoking heroin thing didn't last long, thank fuck. I knew it was bad news but the way I looked at it was that we got it for free - so let's never pay for it. The same went with coke. I was never a big coke head and didn't spend much money on it. I found myself only taking it at a night out when someone was handing it out in the toilet; a wee line here or there and didn't think much about it. Well, apart from keeping me up watching shit TV, drinking a can of beer and thinking this is my last fucking can - isn't this fun. But one night I went round to see Fla - we would always have beer and whisky and he would have a smoke - but out of the blue Fla says, "you want a wee line of coke" and I'm like, "yeah, sure." So he pulls out a bag with a good bit in it and away we go talking shit. You know what I'm talking about? When you're full of the devil's dandruff and giving it, "I'm going to go to the gym, get myself in shape, and what did you say? Do I want another whisky? Yeah, large one mate and turn the sounds up". We sat up till 5 am and I was like, "I need to go home before I get kicked out".

About a week later, just as my hangover was away, I went back round to have a beer with Fla and he says the same thing - "you want a line?".

I'm like, "sure but let me half you for it and he pulls out a block of coke, about three grand of the stuff, and hands it to me. I licked it. I don't know why, I'd just never seen that much coke before and my lips and tongue went numb.

Fla went, "I'm looking after it for some cunt, that's all you need to know, mate, so help yourself".

After a few weeks of popping round for a beer and a few lines the demons started to pay me a visit. Fucking hell, where is the fun in this, I'm thinking. Time to walk away. The guy Fla was watching the coke for didn't pay him so Fla didn't give it back. Simple as that. You're no' paying me, then fuck you! I'm keeping your coke. After a few weeks he sold it, made some good money, and I told him, it was just like back in 1995 with the smack - we had our fun and walked away.

Out of all the years of drug taking that, I'm sure, was the only time it was free. We loved smoking hash but really we paid for it in more ways than one. Brian was hiding from all of the drug dealers in Penilee because he never paid his tick bill. If he got money one of us would have to go and buy it for him. We did more tapping then Fred Astaire and were in more debt than Ethiopia. We would get our hash on tick all week, pay the dealers on a Friday night, then have to tick more the next day. One night Brian was having a party. It had been going on for days and we'd ticked every dealer in town, but we had £20 in cash so we had to find a new dealer who we could buy from. A guy sitting in the party said he knew about a guy round at the flats.

We asked, "is he cool?"

"Yeah," he says, "my brother goes to him all the time".

So me and Wullie go round with this guy to the flats in Penilee (they are all gone now, thank fuck). We didn't know the chap on the door but when he opens the door he goes, "who the fuck are yous cunts?"

We let our new pal do all the talking. So the guy says, "go into the kitchen. I'll tell Big Tam you're here". As we're walking into the flat we see it's mobbed full of guys and girls drinking and smoking. We're standing in the kitchen waiting when Tam and about five other guys walk in, all armed with knives and I'm thinking 'fucking great'.

So Tam says to our new pal, "how d' you know I'm dealing?"

"My brother, Ian, comes here for his hash" our pal replies.

So Tam says, "your brother owes me a lot of fucking money and I'm going to take it out on yous".

So I'm like, "hey, we just met this cunt at a party. We don't know him. We were just wanting a smoke".

And Tam says, "who the fuck are yous?"

Wullie tells him who he is, and who his brother is, and the guy says "OK, you can go".

And Wullie says, "no' without him. He's my best mate. If he stays then I stay".

Tam thinks about it for a minute and then says, "OK, both of yous get to fuck out".

Our new pal is like, "can I go, too?" and I'm like, "you'd better ask Tam".

"No," was Tam's blunt reply.

We walked out the kitchen, got to the door, then I turned back.

Wullie was like, "where you fucking going?"

I knocked on the kitchen door. A guy looked out and I said, "can we still buy a bit of hash from you".

He went, "sure, see one of the girls in the living room".

We got our hash walked out the door, onto the street and looked at each other thinking 'did that just happen?' You know what? No one out of all the boys ever saw that wee guy again. I mean, they didn't kill him, but I think he got that much of a kicking he never came back around.

Big Gerry Law once said the best way to get someone out of your life is to loan them money and he was so right. I mean, if someone in the pub is a right cunt and you loan him £20 and then he avoids you, then that's £20 well spent. The sad part about my story is that I gave Brian money and he didn't pay it all back. We fell out; I was pissed off at him because I knew he had the money but if he paid me back then he would have been skint. All my pals lived this way. They would get hash on tick, then pay it back then tick another bit of hash. Or they would take the money they had and go to Govan to buy a bit of hash because they owed the drug dealers in Penilee. I never did tic. I always paid my way. If I didn't have any money then I would tap my mum or dad. I didn't want to get into it with any drug dealers. I mean, they were all good guys and that was their living so I would respect that and pay them up front. The only down side was that they would always dig me about Brian owing them money and tell me, "when you see him, tell him I'm looking for him". I would always just say, "look, nothing to do with me, and the fucker owes me money, too".

Looking back now I loved Brian. His life might have been crazy but he was always the life and soul of the party, and he had a sick sense of humour. One time we took two girls back to my house. I got Brian in the toilet, gave it the 'just a minute girls, we need to talk,' I told him to have a beer, smoke a joint and don't fuck this up. He was like, "OK".

I'm like, "I'm telling you, no crazy shit".

So we walk back into the room, get the girls a drink, offer them a smoke and I put on some music. All good. Then the next song that comes on is the Eagles 'Take it Easy' and the first line they sing is

Well, I'm runnin' down the road tryna loosen my load
I've got seven women on my mind

and as am asking the girls about what they want to do for a living Brian hits out with, "you know I always thought he was singing 'I'm running down the road trying to empty my load!'"

I'm like, 'night, night' - thanks a lot mate . The only good thing was we ran out of skins and Brian went to the all night garage to get more and never came back. So me and the two posh chicks spent the night in my bed. God I miss the nineties.

Around about that time we were all hanging in Scott 'n' Stuart's and Brian came up with the plan to do a bit of armed robbery - you know like, curry shops or ice cream vans. I had to tell him it doesn't matter if it's a van or a bank, you'll get the same jail time, dick-head, but he didn't give a fuck. It was easy money, so without telling us, he robbed the ice cream van, got about £80 and he got away with it. So then he had a taste for it. Then one day Wullie showed up out of the blue with a pocket full of cash and says, "let's go and get drunk".

We went to the Argosy and as we were sitting enjoying a cold beer I asked him where he got the money from.

He says, "you don't want to know," so I'm like, "OK, fine".

Then my dad walks in gets a beer and sits down and says, "the barmaid just told me they got robbed last night. Two young guys with a shotgun".

My heart stopped. I turned and looked at Wullie and he's busy drinking his pint and looking at the sky. I'm thinking, fuck no! But then he looked back at me and I knew it was him and Brian. I'm thinking like, we need to go to another pub quick. We went to the Pines Bar and he told me all about it. Him and Brian waited till it was closing time and everyone was out of the pub and then they ran in with masks on and two bars in a sack to look like a shotgun to scare the shit out of the staff with. Wullie said Brian was on top of the bar going nuts and as they waited for the staff to put the money in the bag Brian grabbed a bottle of whisky and started to drink it. Then they got the bag of money and ran out of the pub, down the back lane, through a few back streets and jumped a taxi. I mean, a fucking taxi! Who uses a taxi as a getaway car? They got the taxi to Wullie's mum's flat, gave the guy a good tip, sat and split the cash and then they had a beer before Brian heads out into the night. So Wullie came to find me. I gave him a hard time in the Pines and he was like, "I'm buying you drink, stop being a cunt". They got about two grand and they got away with it. And I think that was the last time they were pals. After that they didn't get on. I think it was something Wullie wanted to forget, as nuts as he was, but for Brian, he was just getting warmed up. Wullie told me, and I was thinking who would Brian tell? And the only person I could think of was Stuart. Him and Brian had been best pals for years.

A few weeks later me Brian and Stuart got hold of some acid. We tripped all night, drinking and smoking and the sounds on it were great. I loved LSD. Then as the sun was coming up our acid trip was coming down and the three of us were all sitting chilling after a long mad night. Anyone who has taken LSD will tell you the next day you feel like you've been at T in the Park for the weekend. You feel dirty, in need of a long hot bath; even just sitting in a room all night you still feel like you've been away, and you have – it's just that you've been away in your head. That's why they call it a trip - that and you don't know if you're going to make it back, you know, like a bad trip. I never got a bad trip once and was sure those who did the most shouting about a bad trip were just attention seeking cunts. Anyway, that early morning we were just talking and smoking a wee joint before we went our ways, maybe it was the effect of the acid, but I started to think they were saying shit about the pub robbery. You know, trying to be smart thinking I don't know so will never work out what they're on about.

So I tell them," I'm no one's cunt. I know what yous are on about". They both start to look at each other wondering what I'm going on about.

Stuart looks lost and says, "I don't know what you mean, mate".

And I'm like, "look it's five in the morning I'm no' getting into it, OK".

Stuart says, laughing, "into what?"

I started to get pissed off and turned to Brian and said, "yeah, big fucking deal. You and Wullie robbed the Argosy".

Brian says, "that's bullshit".

I go, "don't try and lie. He told me all about how yous got a taxi for the getaway, and when you split the money you ripped a £20 note in half and said when we've spent all this we'll meet up tape this back together, and get drunk with it".

Stuart is now in shock. He says to Brian, "is this true?"

Brian looked at me and says, "Wullie has a big fucking mouth on him".

Stuart kicked the table up in the air and all the beer and fag ash goes everywhere. At this point I'm thinking ,OK, maybe they weren't talking about the pub. Once the table came back to earth Stuart jumped over it and attacked Brian and I'm in the middle of them trying to fix the mess I've made. Turns out that Brian hadn't told anyone. It was only Wullie who had told me. Well to be fair he had to because I was drinking the money with him, but what pissed Stuart off was that weeks before the robbery Stuart and Brian were planning it together. They went over it a million times to make sure they got it right; Stuart wasn't daft he didn't want to do time inside so they ran over it every night. The plan was all set; they just had to pick the right night to get it done. Then they were going away to Spain, get some summer work and stay out in the sun for as long as they could. But the part that went wrong was that Brian got drunk with Wullie one night and told him all about it, and knowing Wullie he would have had pound signs in his eyes. They just got drunk that night and did it and got away with it.

Brian's luck was only going to last so long. He was getting away with too much and sooner or later he was going to pop up on the radar; all the robberies, all the drug runs, were going to catch up with him. Eventually, one night he went to rob the all-night garage but the guy didn't hand over anything and Brian ran off, but on his way home through Penilee he saw a window was open in the community centre so he jumped in. Turns out it was open because some cunt had already broken into it and now Brian is in there with the cops on the way. So he grabs a big tube of sweets and jumps back out the window and eats the sweet as he walks home drunk. When he got home he went straight to bed and about twenty minutes later the cops bang on the door. They had followed a trail of sweets round to his front door and they found Brian in his bed, hugging a tube of sweets in a drunken sleep.

The next day I get a phone call about it so headed round and Brian's dad opened the door.

I said, "is it true".

"Yeah, Joe. The cops have him".

I'm like, "how did they know where he lived?

And his dad says, "because fucking Hansel left a trail for them".

The cops soon matched Brian's finger prints to all the other shit and he got four years inside. When your pal gets the jail it wakes you up. It makes you realise how easy it is if you fuck about. And it also makes you no' ever take your freedom for granted to have a beer or a joint or go out for dinner with your girlfriend, because your pal is stuck in a cold dark cell counting the stars and the hours.

Brian was that one pal that everyone has or should have whose life is crazy, but he is the life and soul of the party. He knows how to enjoy himself, just maybe too much was the problem, but the one thing I knew was out of us all if anyone could survive jail it was him. I mean, Wullie and Fla could, too, they were tough fuckers who wouldn't take any shit but Brian wasn't like that. He was happy-go-lucky fit into anywhere so I knew he would make pals and get up to no good with them in there. Me, I couldn't do time. As I always said, I'm too pretty for the jail; and Brian did back that up – he said to me years later that they would sell my wee skinny ass for a packet of tobacco, so fuck that! The four years passed in no time - well for us, no' Brian - but when he got out we had a party for I was looking forward to seeing him. I felt bad when he was inside. We scattered to the wind. I didn't see any of the boys for months, maybe even a year or two. None of us went to visit him which was unforgivable as pals go but when you're young you don't think about shit like that. You just think about yourself.

So party night was good and busy. Brian hadn't seen any of us for years but we hadn't either so it was good to see the old gang back for one night only. Thinking back now, the next day the four of us all went to the Argosy and that was the last day we would all be together at the same time. I wish someone had a photo of that day or even a photo of the four

125

of us together. I don't think there's one anywhere. So we sat and drank and laughed not knowing it was the last day we had together and as the day went on Fla and Wullie left and it was just me and Brian sitting late into the night, just like old times. I had to ask him now it was just us, what was it really like inside? He said the first week was hell but you just keep your head down and get into the routine of prison life. You can tell who are the neds the cunts who just want to make a name for themselves so you just stay out of their way and let the screws deal with them.

I said, "how do they deal with them?"

This is the story he told me.

Some wee guy comes in thinking he's hard because one of his brothers had done this or that, so the screws just put him in with someone who is doing life, like Grossberger, nicknamed after the big guy in Stir Crazy. I'm sitting thinking this is no going to end well. So the young hardman who is giving the screws a hard time gets moved into Grossberger's cell and that night as they're talking Grossberger doesn't tell the wee ned he is doing life. No, what he tells him is he has three months to go, same as the wee ned. He says when he gets out him and a pal have a job lined up and they stand to make about three million from it, if all goes well that is. So the wee ned's ears are up like a Doberman hearing a burglary. Grossberger says, there's just one problem. We need a third man, someone who's skinny and can fit through the factory window because his pal is as fat as him.

So the wee ned is like, "I'll do it, I'll fit through the

window".

And Grossberger is like, "I don't know if you would fit".

Now in the jail in your wee cell you have a chair like a school chair and Grossberger says to the wee ned, "I tell you what. If you can fit through the back of that chair you're sitting on then I'll phone my pal tomorrow and tell him I have a guy who will fit through the window.

And the ned goes, "OK" and makes his way through the chair, but as he gets half way through it Grossberger, who is gay by the way, knocks the wee cunt out cold and then has his way with him all night and then some more before breakfast. When the screws open the cell door the prisoners aren't sitting smoking in bed after a romantic night. No. the wee ned is sat in the corner with his head down and for a change he doesn't have anything to say.

So the screw asked him, "are we going to get any more trouble from you?"

The ned doesn't even look up. He just says, "no boss".

"OK," says the screw, "away back to your own cell".

As he runs out Grossberger shouts, "call me".

That day in the pub I said you should go round all the schools in Glasgow and tell that story and the city would be full of fucking angels .

So life was going good. Me and my girlfriend had a got a flat. We were both in good jobs, we had two cats, and at the weekends we went to the video shop and spent our weekends having a beer and a few joints. I was taking it easy on the hash. I could never smoke it every day anyway; it didn't work for me the way it did for others, and as my old man would say, 'if you drink and smoke hash every day like me you'll have nothing to look forward too on your days off'. So I was in a good place in my early twenties. Every now and again I would have a smoke late at night and wonder how all my pals were doing because none of them were drinking in the pub. It was just me going down to see my dad and the boys once a week on a day off, then I would be back at work. One day I was just home from work when my mum phoned. She said Wullie had been at the door looking for me and he was on his way to my flat. I hadn't seen him in about a year and it felt like forever. He showed up with a wee bag of Valium and a big bag of beers. This was the day we worked out a code for my buzzer so I would know it was him at my door. Wullie was happy to see me and I was, too. It was good to see one of my pals because I had just run off into the night and hadn't seen any one of them for a few years.

Wullie was celebrating. He was a dad, the first of us to become a father.

I'm like, "fuck me, that's a big deal".

And he was like, "yeah, let's get drunk".

We took a Valium, had a few cans, then Wullie was on the phone to his old pal from Renfrew. He came to pick us up in his dad's car; his parents were on holiday. We got to his house and it was really nice, like nothing me and Wullie were brought up in: big driveway, four bedrooms, two bathrooms, big back garden. When we walked in the house was jumping but it was only girls, there were no guys, not that we had a problem with that, and we knew Wullie's pal was just trying to show off. But me and Wullie were no' interested in any of the girls - we were there to drink and smoke and maybe chase all the birds away by playing The Stones and Pink Floyd. Wullie's pal says another guy was showing up soon and some of the girls were going and we were like, "cool". I was offered a tour of the house and when you're on Valium anything sounds fun, even a shit tour. He showed me the table in the dining room and said, "this is an antique, been in my family for years," and I'm like, "cool" as Wullie is giving me another Valium.

So some of the girls pissed off and this guy shows up full of coke. Now Wullie is talking to the girls about being a dad in the kitchen and I'm just sitting playing The Stones, smoking and drinking, when the coke-head gets up and changed the record to some shit dance music and sits back down. He just looks at me as if to say 'you have a problem?' So I get up, put my beer and joint down on the table - you know how to put a joint on a table you have the lit end over the side - and I changed the music back to The Stones, sit back down and look at the coke-head like, 'let's do this, fucker'. Just as I sat down Wullie walks in and sits down beside the guy, and I reach for my beer and remember it's on the table. As I got back up I remember my joint was on that fucking antique table, too. I looked down and the joint was done. It had burned the table. I was, like, 'it's time to do the right thing and leave the room and let Wullie or the cokehead take the blame'. When I left the coke-head says to Wullie, "your pal is getting it". Wullie asked "why" that's when the guy bit his glass and burst his lip, and Wullie being Wullie didn't take any chances, just hit him with a bottle of beer. The two of them were rolling about the floor.

When I went to run back in they were up against the door and I couldn't get to Wullie to back him up, but then he shouted, "keep pushing the door, I've got his head against it". The coke-head got put out the front door and ran into the night. As a matter of fact everyone left apart from me and Wullie, even the guy whose parents owned it went to his birds house, and we just sat drinking, smoking and talking shit like old times. When we woke up in the morning, well afternoon, we couldn't remember why we were partying in the first place. All we knew was we had to try and clean this guy's house up a bit and get the fuck out. As we were cleaning Wullie stuck the Hoover in a pint of beer and it blew up.

I was, like, "time to go - the pubs will be open" and Wullie went, "wait a minute. I know why we were celebrating, it's because I became a dad last night. I need to get to the hospital for visiting time".

Wullie would do anything to get money for a good time. Thing is, all my pals well most of them, would. They could never just accept that fact that they're skint today so just stay in and watch TV.

I remember one time in the pub there was a wee guy watching the races and I said, "I take it you have a bet on.

He says, "if this fucker comes in I'm out all weekend getting drunk".

"What if it doesn't?" I asked.

He said, "I'll be watching The X Factor with ma maw.

When I was about 21 I had my own flat and Wullie would always pop up when he had falling out with his girlfriend. He would press the buzzer six times so I knew it was him.

He pressed it that much he kept breaking the fucking thing. I would open the door and just go and sit down. He would walk into the kitchen and put beers in the fridge and pour one for him and me without even saying "hello". He'd hand me a drink and just go off on one about his life, but one night I opened the door went and sat down and he was taking so long to get up the stairs I went to have a look and he was on his knees fighting for breath. I got him into the flat and he told me he had robbed a bus with a knife. The driver handed him a bag of coins and he ran off with it into a school by climbing over a 20 foot fence. He fell from the top of it and his ribs landed on the bag of coins. He had about £50 in pound coins in it. I told him, "you need a doctor" but he handed me the bag and said, "no, I need a drink". He was fucking nuts risking his life or jail for fifty bucks.

Another time he came to see me was just at Christmas and he had a bag full of Christmas cards. He had walked around a few streets putting his hand in all the post boxes that were full with the Christmas rush and took out as many cards as he could get his hands on. He opened them - about forty cards and got about £20; a few wee grandkids didn't get there £10 from granny that year. Then he asked me if I had any spare Christmas cards so he could fuck with people's minds - you know, if the card said 'Merry Christmas to Bill and Jean from Jim and Jill', well Wullie took a new card and wrote 'to Jean, Merry Christmas, I want to suck your big tits, love Jim, and a Happy New Year' and put it back in its original envelope and back in the post box.

All the years we ran about trying to get by I always worked.

My wee maw always made sure I had a job and wasn't sitting about doing fuck all like my pals, so if I wanted a few days off without losing my job I had to phone in sick and then the hard part, get a sick line from the doctor. Over the past 20 years I should have won about ten academy awards for my acting in the doctor's office. One time I hit my wee toe off a door in my flat; I just had socks on and the door came running back to shut and took my wee toe with it. It was so bad all I could do was scream in silence. My toe was bruised pretty badly so I phoned in sick, but a few days later I had to see the doctor to get a sick line and I was going for a four week line so I got a pen, coloured my wee toe in with black ink, and rubbed it in with my fingers. It worked a treat; it was that good the doctor was going to send me to A&E. He gave me my four week line and as I was walking out of his office I saw him looking at his pen - he was thinking it had burst because he had ink on his fingers. I must be losing my touch because the last sick line I went to get I ended up getting my prostate checked. I remember lying there going great but I went too far and so did the doctor. As I was lying there with the docs finger in my prison pocket I kept thinking if a guy with a white coat and a cup of tea walks in here and says what the fuck are yous two doing in my office I will go fucking nuts. I walked home that day with no sick line, just an ass full of K Y jelly. He didn't even wipe my bum, just did what he had to and sent me away like a cheap fucking hooker.

Wullie knew how to play the system. We went to the dole office to get a hardship loan.

He says, "tell them you need new stuff for your flat, like

a carpet and a fridge, and if you ask for £400 you should get about half". So as we were waiting Kenny, a guy Wullie knew, asked us what we were up to. We tell him and he fills in the form. After we've all been seen we get outside.

"Right, how much did you get?" Wullie £250, me £200, Kenny fuck all.

We were like, "what? How come you got nothing? What did you say you needed?"

And Kenny says "I told them I needed a wee holiday, a wee bit of time away".

"OK, good to see you, Kenny," and we are away to the pub - "bye".

Like every gang of young lads you have to grow up unless you're in a rock band, so we all did what everyone else did, drifted along from day to day. You get busy with some wee bird or a job, or doing time. When I moved out of Penilee in '96 I got a flat with my girlfriend at the time, and she got me off my lazy stoned ass. You know what it's like. When you're stoned, talking about all the things you want to do in life like go to see The Rolling Stones or Pink Floyd, then someone would say let's get tickets to see them, but then you would just spend the money on more hash. Well my girlfriend would make me move off my butt and go. So we went to gigs and went on holiday and looking back now they are some great memories, a lot better than sitting in my mum's back bedroom, stoned.

One year we went away to Spain for two weeks. I asked my dad to look after our two cats, Mick and Keith, and he did but he had his mates up after the pub shut, and when one of

133

my neighbours came to the door to ask him to keep it down he offered her a drag of his joint and told her to chill out. I mean, talk about back to front, me coming home to tell my dad off for having a party. I was like, "you should be keeping an eye on me, I'm 21 you're 53, for fuck sake. But going on holiday was the best. I loved being away in the sun, drinking beer by the pool, watching the topless girls walk past through my sunglasses. I was like the Terminator looking for Sarah Connor. One day we went on a day trip to Gibraltar which was a good day out apart from getting stuck on the bus beside some couple, and the wife wouldn't shut the fuck up the whole way there. She told us about every fucking holiday she had been on. When the bus stopped we made a run for it to get away from them. The first thing we had to do was pick up stamps for my girlfriend's dad and when we walked into the post office there were two queues - one short and one as long as the fucking island - we had a fight about waiting or going so she waited and I went and found a pub. About an hour later she found me. It wasn't hard - she just had to look for the Tennent's sign. Three days later we went away again; this time we went to Morocco for the day. The journey was a killer - up at 4am, on the bus. And guess who was on the bus? Yep, the boring couple from a few days ago. Then it was onto the ferry for a few hours, and it didn't have a bar so by the time we got to Africa I was needing a beer. We walked down off the ferry to get our passports stamped and when the guy did mine he missed half of it. I went to say to him what he had done but he just moved me on and says, "it's OK". The day out was amazing. I was walking about thinking I was Indiana

Jones, just that I was looking for the holy grail full of beer. At the end of the tour they took us to a restaurant for everyone to eat in - except for me, because I got lost from the tour. When the tour guy found me he took me to the restaurant through the back door and when he opened it a cat ran out and it was in a fucking hurry so I just stuck with the beer. Me and my girlfriend got a seat and the boring couple got the two seats beside us. I was like, fucking great! The wife kept going on and on about the food and asking why I didn't want anything to eat? I had a light bulb moment; I said I don't eat food because I have a serious drug habit. She laughed because she didn't know what to say.

So she says, "really?"

I'm like, "yeah, the only reason I was late here was because I was buying heroin - it's in my prison pocket".

She said, "where?"

I said, "it's up my ass, hen".

She didn't talk to us for the rest of the day. Job done. When we got back to the ferry everyone was in line to get their passports checked and when they got to me, you guessed it. They told me to stand at the side. I knew it! This half stamp was no' going to get me back on the ferry.

I got a bit pissed off and told the guard, "you don't understand".

He put his hand on his gun and said, "no, you don't understand".

I was like, "cool big man, you won't get any trouble here". They let everyone on apart from me. All the passengers were looking over the side like I was the guy from Midnight Express.

I could see the boring couple looking and I'm thinking 'she better no' shout it's in his prison pocket, officer'. My tour guide was with me, talking to the guards.

Then he said he was going onto the ferry and I'm like, "are you fuck, mate, if am doing a long weekend here so are you."

Ad he was like, "it's OK, the captain is coming to bring you on".

I'm like, "he better be. I'm too pretty for the jail. They would play cards for me over here".

But the captain came and saved me.

I was sitting in my flat one day and my buzzer went. I knew it was Wullie because he pressed it six times. My old man came up with it - never mind fucking up my buzzer! I did suggest we could have the code four times but I was outvoted by my old man. No its six and that's it so my buzzer goes mad and I know it's Wullie. He walks in looking rough with a bag of cans. "Alright mate? What's happening?" He tells me he's been on it for weeks and last night he kicked off and went mad so one of his fed up neighbours phoned the cops. So Wullie, being full of drugs and drink, goes off on one and he ends up rolling about with the cops, but they charge him and then take him to Levendale Hospital to be sectioned. So Wullie wakes up in the 'dale. He can't remember a thing from the night before and when the nurse gives him his breakfast she tells him he is in the 'dale, and no' the Southern General. He thinks 'shit, what have I done'. The nurse tells him he will need to speak to a specialist before he can get out so he is like, "OK, thanks". He knows he's fucked up and has to play it cool if he wants out. Now the only thing I couldn't work out was we all knew Wullie wasn't right in the head so to be in the 'dale he was in the right place for help, but he wanted out. They took him to a waiting area and told him the psychiatrist would see him soon. As he was sitting waiting there was another patient waiting, too, a big guy with a shaved head, covered in tattoos. He was just sitting across from Wullie looking at him.

He didn't say a word, so Wullie went, "you all right mate?"

The guy just nodded his head, then a few minutes later the big cunt got up, walked over to where Wullie was, sat down beside him, put his hand in his pocket still looking right into Wullie's eyes and pulled out a lollipop.

He said, "do you want a lick?"

Wullie was like, "no thanks mate". His hangover was kicking in and so was the fear. Wullie saw the psychiatrist and the only reason he got out that day was because he told the guy when he woke up he was embarrassed, so the guy says if you're embarrassed then you're not off your head, so you can go, but try and take it easy.

Wullie was like, "sure thing, doc," then straight to the shops for beers and up to mine for a drink.

I asked him, "why didn't you stay and see if they could help you with your demons?"

He said, "fuck that. They were all nuts in there, even the psychiatrist looked mad. The cunt had a hunch, I bet he has a wok so he can iron his shirts. No way was I hanging about. Fuck that".

It was the drugs that was making my pals go mad. I was lucky because I wasn't as strong as my mates so my body would say 'times up, no more of that shit'. Even smoking dope was hard work. Day to day everything was a struggle when you're stoned. and all that white powder will kill you faster than a bullet. The speed bombs were like a cheap man's coke. These wee pills would stop you blinking for three days. We would go out to the pub all day, then go to the dancing at night. still no' drunk. And we didn't even like the fucking dancing!

I remember one morning I was in my pal's house playing with a set of moon chucks at 7am when his dad walked past the room door, up for work and said, "morning Joe". I was like, 'fucking hell, what am I doing? Time to go home'. My mate had some of my pills he had watched for me, so as he is giving me them out from his own bag of pills we decided to swap some - so we are like, "you give me two of them and I'll give you two of these, and give me something to help me sleep, and make sure it's something good. I haven't had a good sleep in days". And as we were trading each other for pills I spy this big white square pill. It was standing out from all the rest shining like a street light on a cold winter night.

I was like, 'hello pretty'. I took that big fucker out of the bag and says to my pal, "can I have this bad boy".

He said "yeah, sure".

I was like, "what is it?"

And he said, "it's a Rennie, mate, for when you have heartburn".

I was like, "fucking hell! I was hoping it was going to take me out of the matrix there".

Thinking back it seems like we were all hanging about

together for years but it was only about a year we were all round at Stuart and Scott's because the same old story - our girlfriend's didn't like each other. That made it hard to hang out, so as time went on we saw less and less of each other. I moved into a flat, Chris was busy being in a relationship, too, Scott was in a band so that kept him away and Stuart was seeing a girl who lived two doors away from him and when his wee mum gave up that big house we all sat in he moved into his girlfriend's house with her mum and her gran. I was living up in Crookston with my soon to be wife and our kids, so I would pop down to see the boys on my days off from work. I would go and see Chris because he was always ready and up for a beer, and you would always find Scott or Stuart or someone in with Chris. His room was known as 'Fla's Bar'. One day I was round there and Chris says, "let's go see if Stuart is in his bird's house". We went round and he told us to come in. He had a spare room like a man cave - P.C, TV, DVD and CD player. We sat about in his room in his girlfriend and mum's house and had a few beers. Later on I asked Chris about Stuart's setup and Chris just said, "he's made himself at home, mate".

Stuart was living with his girlfriend just before his mum moved house, so Chris comes home from a holiday and meets Scott as soon as he gets home from the airport. Chris had plans that night with his girlfriend to go out, so as him and Scott head out with a bag of beers he tells his girlfriend, "I won't be long," and him and Scott walk round to see Stuart. As they walk down the road Chris was telling Scott all about his holiday, you know, how good the weather was and how cheap the beer is. As they got to the door Scott says, "I'm going into my mum's to get my other jacket," and Chris says, "OK, see you in a minute". Chris heads in to see Stuart who is sitting in the front room with his girlfriend's little brother. He sits down, says "hi" to Stuart, his girlfriend and her brother when there's a loud knock at the door. Stuart looks out the window and Chris says, "is that Scott," and Stuart goes white and says, "no, it's the fucking cops". Chris is still on his first sip of beer when the cops burst in to raid the house. Turns out Stuart was now the guy in the street watching drugs for someone. The cops got everyone in the one room; the grandmother and the mother of the house, everyone. There's another knock at the door and it's Scott. The cops tell him to fuck off and Scott being smart, he did. The cops didn't want to hear what Stuart had to say about the drugs being his, they wanted to make an example of the whole household. They were given a sheet of paper to read, like, their rights, and what was going to happen and then they were taken into a room one by one. Chris took the sheet, opened a beer and started to read it. One of the cops says, "don't open that beer," and Chris says, "I can do what I want until you arrest me," so he drank his beers and read the sheet, then read it again because it was his turn to go into the room. Chris pissing off the cops didn't play out too well for him because out of everyone in the house only he got the finger up the bum search for wasting their time. When the cops were done talking to everyone the whole house got taken to spend the night in the cells, and Chris missed his night out. After all that Stuart and his girlfriend were done for possession and he moved out of Penilee, just like me and Scott had.

Now Chris was the only one in our gang who never left the scheme .We would always meet at Fla's Bar when we could, but growing up keeps you busy. I missed that wee gang of pals and it's sad that most of them are now behind the sun. I would love it if they were all still about, getting on with their lives and we could just meet up now and then for a beer, and talk about all the fun times; like when Brian said he wasn't a criminal because he had only been to jail once and I said, "you only need to shag one sheep to be a sheep shagger". Or the time we were in a pub in town and I asked the barmaid when her next day on was, and she had a stutter and went, "Tue Tue Tue Tuesday," and Chris says, "is there a cat in here?" I burst out laughing and she told us all to, "get ou ou out". Or the time me, Fla, Scott and Stuart were talking to a big fat guy in the pub and he says the doctors are giving him a hard time about his weight, and he says, "obesity runs in my family," and I went, "mate I think you will find that no cunt runs in your family, that's the problem". The big fucker went nuts so we were told to get out again - no wonder we spent so much time in Fla's bar. We were barred everywhere else.

MAN TAKES
A DRINK,
THEN DRINK
TAKES THE MAN.

CHAPTER 5

Even Wine Drinkers Die.

All things must past and in 2005, that was the year my life would change forever and the pub would never be the same. On the 31st of January me and Trish went to the pub for the New Year. I had arranged to meet my old man. I told him, "don't get drunk, I'll be down and we can have a drink with each other at the bells thinking it would be good because over the years with a divorce in the family we couldn't remember the last time we had spent the New Year together. It was only four years before this that I was sitting with him on Christmas Eve at midnight and into Christmas Day and he said, "this is the first time in a long time I've been with one of my sons on Christmas Day, so I'm thinking, 'get my dad in the pub and celebrate New Year together'. Happy days, but when I walked in and saw him I knew he was drunk, and my old man was a bad drunk. That's why I drank in the pub in the day time because by 7 o'clock my old man would be pissed and looking for an argument.

As me and Trish walked over I asked him to slide up so me and Trish could sit together and he says, "I've been sitting here all day, why do I need to move".

I was like, "fine it's, OK, we'll sit at the bar".

My dad walked out and I went after him. I told him, "I asked you not to get drunk. You could have had a good night with us," but he didn't want to know.

He made out that I didn't want to be seen sitting with him and I said, "that's the hash talking, then." As he walked away I said, "you know some night we will do this as we always do, but one day it will be for the last time and we won't ever see each other to say sorry, and one of us will never get over it," but he just kept walking.

A week later my grandmother phoned. She had been trying to get hold of me. My dad had had a heart attack on the third. I got to the hospital and he was telling me he was OK and kept going on about a bottle of Jack Daniel's he had got me and it was in his flat, telling me to take his keys and get it. I'm like, "fuck that. Are you OK" and he was saying, "yeah, I'm fine". I knew the bottle of Jack was his way of saying sorry; old Glasgow guys can't say sorry to your face. The doctor told me my dad needed an op. He had a blood clot near his heart and would get it done on the 14th. So on that day I noticed a missed call on my phone and I'm thinking 'that's him had his op. That was quick'. But it was a nurse saying to get down here as soon as you can. My heart sank. I knew my dad was gone but my mind wouldn't take it in. I think it took me about 40 minutes to get there when it really only takes me 20 minutes any other time. The doctor sat me down and told me my dad was gone. It broke my heart and put me in a world of pain to think he was gone forever. I sat with him to say goodbye, then Trish came to pick me up. She says, "who will you tell first, Joe or your gran?" And then it hit me. I had to go and tell a mother she had lost her son and a guy he had lost his brother. Fucking hell, I don't need this!

I was feeling alone. My two brothers lived down south so I had to deal with it all till my brother Gerry showed up about three days later, gave me a hug and said, "I'm here now. We can do this together". They say you should always find the good in a bad situation and it was hard with this one, except for the past few years Trish was wanting to have another kid and I was always like, "yeah. maybe someday. I mean, I have Shawnay, what's the hurry," but after my dad passed I kept thinking if I go I don't want Shawnay to feel alone the way I did. I want her to have a brother or sister to get through it together and on the 25th of May 2006 Lucas Arthur Reavey was born.

After my dad died the gang in the pub all went fast. It was like the end of a mafia film; maybe it was just all the boys were getting on a bit. Drinking and smoking dope everyday won't help but I was 29, when my old man passed and over the next few years, I would lose a lot of good pals, but I guess that's the way it goes when your pals are twenty or thirty years older than you. When someone you love dies you fill your mind with 'ifs'; you know, 'if only I had done this, 'if only he had stopped doing that'. I said to Gerry Law about it one day, thinking if maybe my dad had stopped smoking and drinking so much whisky, and maybe just stuck to the wine he would still be here, and Gerry said, "there's a lot of wine drinkers in the graveyard, Joe".

With my dad now gone I knew the Argosy would no' be the same, but I knew it was the best place to be to get over losing my old man, to just sit with his pals, a bunch of guys all missing the same guy I was. That's what got me through the first few weeks. We would talk about him and how he would make us listen to Elvis, and how he would say Elvis didn't die - he just went home. At this time most of the guys were away from the pub and it was only me and Gerry on week days; most guys were at work but I had week days off; being a chef I worked weekends. I always thought big Gerry had the best job in the world being a money lender. I mean, as a young kid I would think, one day I would love to do that job, but I knew you had to be a hard man to do it because if you gave out money people need to be scared of you, or they won't pay you back. As I got older I knew why Gerry was fed up most of the time. I mean, think about it, he was sitting in a pub drinking a bottle of Coke and listening to guys explaining why they can't pay him this week, sitting there with every gambler and his drunk brother bullshitting him on why they can't pay - same old shit, day in day out 24/7. And he would only drink maybe once a week because sitting in the pub seven days a week it could be too handy to think, fuck it, just have a wee beer - then before you know it you're drunk and you don't know who tapped you money. But that did happen a lot, many a Saturday afternoon I would be describing the guy who came in last night and tapped £20 off him.

Taking drugs in the pub was no big deal; everyone was doing it. Some guys would take speed to keep them going or a bit of coke at the weekends and everyone was smoking hash. There was more joints getting smoked then cigarettes, but for me it was LSD every weekend. Me and Wullie would trip out of our heads up in the lounge. The place was jumping with drunks, speed freaks, all out to party and we would be in the middle of it like two ghosts. We would just trip, drink beer and smoke everyone's hash till chucking out time. Looking back now it gives me the fear how I survived. A few years before my dad passed we became pals with Al. He wasn't long off smack so a lot of the boys didn't take to him, but he was sound and would do anything for you. He looked real badass with the top of his two ears bitten off, but he became my pal and I didn't let anyone touch him, apart from Rab Fraser. He would take the piss out of Al and if Rab takes the piss out of you then you're on your own. I would just make fun of it and after Rab had a rant at him I would say, "you taking that? Wouldn't be me but I'm just saying," and Al would say, "shut up, brother, he's going to kill me". Al called everyone brother.

As the years rolled on everyone ended their friendship with drugs. I mean you can't do it forever. For me it was no more LSD and hash. It was getting too much, even just trying to buy a round of drinks was fucking hard work and I'm thinking this is no' right, it's only a fucking round. Time to knock it on the head. I've seen guys going downhill fast with drink or drugs. One day I was sitting in the pub and this young girl came in with a black eye and tells her dad at the next table that a guy had punched her. He was mad and says, "get his name and address and I'll go up tomorrow and deal with him". So about a week later I sit down with a pint and that same guy is sitting at the next table, mad drunk. I say to him, "how did you get on with the cunt who hit your kid?" and he says, "who hit my kid?" I remember thinking that I hope I don't turn out to be a dad like that for my kids.

So no more cheap pills from Al, as much fun as it was it was mad. You would be sitting having a beer about to go home for your tea, then pop one wee pill and me, Gerry and Rab would be sitting till last orders on a week night talking about what songs to play next on the jukebox. You'll have one night in your life when if you're lucky you will say that's it, party's over, and stop all the shit nights like going home and popping a few more pills to keep going, but you don't know if it's New York or New Year. You take the wrong pills, like sleeping pills, and no one can wake you and next thing you know you're In A&E, drinking charcoal to soak up the pills in your gut. Then the next day you've a hangover from hell, you're shitting tar and thinking this is a good fucking laugh. Its moments like that, sitting on the pan, that you will rethink your life.

A few months after my dad had passed away the pub was nuts. We started to get back into drugs like a bit of coke and Es. We were popping Es like fucking Skittles. I was thinking I'm doing this to take my mind off my old man no' being here and maybe Gerry and Rab are doing the same, but it wasn't just at the weekends. It was, like, maybe a Wednesday at 5pm when Gerry and Rab were about to go up the road for their dinner and Al would come in with some good pills and I would say to them, "are you in?" And they would say, "yeah, I'm in". Next thing you know we would be playing the tunes on the jukebox, saying to each other "I love this song", then we would have a hug and work out who was getting the next round of beer in and it must have looked bad. Imagine you're a guy on his way home from work on a Wednesday night, you pop into the pub for a quiet quick pint before you go home to the good lady and there are three guys in the corner hugging, dancing and drinking beer like we were fucking Vikings. You would think this is a mad house, but the pub was always like this. A guy and his wife walked in one afternoon for a wee drink and everyone in the pub was doing 'Row, Row, Row your Boat' sitting on the floor. No one remembers who or why it started but that couple didn't hang about for a second drink. At this time I was thinking I'm getting too old for this, but I was only in my twenties. Guys like Gerry, Rab, Mick and Shug were all in their forties so I was like, if they can do it still, then so can I. My dad never did hard drugs. He didn't like them. He hated coke-heads. He was happy with drink and hash, so maybe it was now that he was gone that we took the pills, because he wasn't there to dig us. Well dig me, anyway.

Just before my dad passed he was sitting in the pub when Al's girlfriend came in looking for him. she asked my dad if he had seen Al and he said no. She says, "I have to meet him here. Can I get a drink and sit with you." He says, "sure," so she went to the bar. My dad was thinking 'what the fuck can I talk to her about? I'm too stoned for this bullshit'. He had a packet of toffee sweets in his pocket and when she sat down he asked her, "would you like a wee sweetie, hen," and she said, "no thanks, I only take them at the weekends".

I was about to turn 30 around about this time. In 2005 and my world was upside down but I didn't know it, I just kept going. With my dad gone I had to look after my old grandmother, get her shopping, make sure she was OK in her flat, and I was a dad to Shawnay. I remember sitting with her in the park thinking this should be the best day of my life staying with my girlfriend and our daughter, but I was stressed and run down from looking after my 90 year old grandmother, and the drink and drugs didn't help. But it was just hard times. It happens in everyone's life when you just get a bad run of things. It was a sad time; my grandmother was heartbroken and my Uncle Joe was, too. He had lost his brother. Joe was in a bad way with the drink before my dad died and when he was gone he just got drunk even more. He would phone and ask me to get him whisky. I felt bad about buying him it; I knew it was killing him but what could I do? He was already too far gone. If I didn't get him it for him he would have hit the D.Ts, or he would have tried to make it to the shops by himself and anything could of happen to him then. So I would take up a bottle and he would need it that bad he would take the first drink out the bottle just to stop him shaking. Then I would get him a glass and roll him a joint and as he sat drinking and smoking I would sit and think about all the good times me, him and my dad had in this flat every Saturday. And now we were on the dark side of life and the party was over.

Everyone loved Joe; he was the friendly neighbourhood postman. He passed away in late 2006. I miss sitting with my dad and Joe in his wee flat. I have some of the best memories of it. He only had three chairs and the one I sat on was a rocking chair. It was so cool to just sit stoned, sipping a beer, listening to The Beatles, Joe's favourite band, and rocking in my rocking chair. Oasis had a song called 'Rockin' Chair' and whenever I hear it my mind goes right back to those Saturday afternoons, sitting laughing with my dad and Joe.

Big Gerry was the next to go. He didn't die; the cops kicked his door in and raided his flat. All the years of money lending had caught up with him. Turns out the cops had been in the pub for several weeks watching all of us, trying to see who was up to what, and it was only Gerry who was making any real money at that time. The only guy in the pub who worked it out was Rab Fraser. He said, "the cops are in here watching us". He could see them with his eyes shut but no one paid any attention to it; most of us were thinking he was stoned and paranoid. The day after Gerry got lifted he was on the front page of the Daily Record. I remember getting a bus to work and seeing Chris Fla standing outside the shops with a mad look on his face, reading the paper, and I was thinking 'what's up with him'. Then I got to my work and saw Gerry's picture on the front cover. Gerry got a few years and they took over a hundred grand off him. The only thing they let him keep was his flat. The judge said it would just cost them more money if they made you homeless after his sentence. The cops were making an example of him to put the fear in all the money lenders in Glasgow, letting them know time was up, the party was over. The Daily Record was running a 'shop a loan shark' campaign. I mean, what chance would you have as a money lender if when someone owed you a few bucks, they could just phone the hotline and you're done, and they don't even need to pay you back. The Daily Record made out that Gerry was a real cunt, but that was bullshit. I knew the guy for 20 years - he was my dad's pal. I would watch him when I was younger doing his thing and he would make sure the guys who were tapping him would still have money for a beer. They would get £10 and a week later pay him back £12, and when they paid him back he would say, "here get yourself a drink" and give them the price of a pint back. Gerry and Rab Donnelly got done over the money lending by the Daily Record but Rab didn't get caught by the cops - it was the Record that went after him. The guy who was writing for the Record phoned the pub one day and asked Rab for his side of the story and Rab said, "come on down to the pub and I'll give you it". But the guy didn't show up - shocker!

Before the days of mobile phones if your good lady was looking for you she phoned the pub's pay phone and one day Rab D was going to the toilet when the phone rang, so he picked it up and says, "hello, Argosy Bar. It was his wife. She said, "is Rab Donnelly in," and Rab shouts out, "is there a Rab Donnelly in the bar," and someone shouts back "no!!" Rab D was always in the pub, day and night, but he never looked drunk. One night a new barmaid says he was no' getting anymore drink so Rab puts his arm on the bar and says, "if I don't get a drink then no cunt is getting one," so the barmaid says, "what do you mean?" and Rab walked along the full bar with his arm on it spilling all the drinks as he passed them. The next day he was back in the pub having a drink. Nowadays you would be barred for life for that – how things have changed.

I haven't seen Gerry Law for years now. He never came back to the pub after his time inside. He became a town drinker. Me and Shug Boyle went and found him in the town and had a drink with him, but that was the last time we saw him. The day after the cops got Gerry I remember walking into the Argosy and the only guy sitting in the corner was Rab Fraser. I was at the bar waiting to get a beer and looking over at the empty corner thinking the party's over, Joe. Me and Rab sat having a drink. He told me it didn't matter if Gerry got time or not, the brewery wouldn't be letting him back in the pub. I was sitting looking around the pub thinking about back in the day with all the boys over the years, and now it was all gone. I miss the walking in and there was always someone in to have a drink with. I miss the madness of a Friday night after work. I miss a Sunday come down but what I miss the most is the Oregon trail, going for a walk through Rosshall park on a sunny day, with a bottle of wine. My dad, Gerry Law and Pat Fla started that walk and in 2005 me and Chris Fla ended it. We were the last two to do it. We did it to say goodbye to my dad and Chris's brother, Andy. We got a bottle of Eldorado and as we were standing on the bridge drinking it I said to Chris, "this tastes so good, why did we ever stop drinking it" and then about 2am and ten pints later I was hugging the pan like it was the love of my life and thinking 'now I remember'.

All the Fla's had left the pub one by one over the years. Andy Fla fell off a chair he was standing on and fell into a table full of empty classes and did a lot of damage to his arm. After that we didn't see much of the brothers. Only Mark and Pat would still pop in, and Pat still does to this day. One of the last of the Mohicans, he is in the 9 o'clock gang, as I call them - a few of the boys who all show up at 9pm. I mean, the pub shuts at 11, that's no' much time to drink beer, but they still do a good job of it.

I couldn't. I need a good six hours to drink beer, maybe I'm just too slow, or like I said before, I'm a greedy fucker. Andy Fla passed away the same year as my dad, 2005; the drink got him. Another good guy gone. After that Chris Fla never came to the Argosy and that pissed me off. I would always try and get him out for a beer but he just didn't want to go to the Argosy, and after a few years I had to look at it from his point of view – maybe it brought back too many memories. I never thought of it that way; I just wanted my pal beside me in the pub. Three of my pals my own age who all drank in the pub with me are all gone now. William Brown died at the age of 27 - God he was a crazy kid. I 'm sure I could do a full book on him and his mad life. Well, maybe one day.

Wullie would just always want to get drunk and high. He should have been a rock star; he could play the guitar and the drums with his eyes shut. He was one of those guys who could just pick up a guitar and play the song on the radio like he'd been playing it for years. I remember one time I spent a week trying to learn a Stones' song I had the book showing me the chords to the song. I kept playing the song over and over but still couldn't get it. Then Wullie pops in to go for a beer and I go to the bathroom to get washed, come back out and he is playing the whole song on the guitar like it was nothing. He just said this song is so cool, and I just said, "bastard". Wullie was a true friend, a good pal. A lot of people didn't take to him because he was wild but if he was your pal he would back you up anytime. He never backed down from a fight and he was the only one of us to join the '27 club'. Chris was always pissed at that. Wullie and his girlfriend Roseann had a son. They lived together for years and if it wasn't for Roseann I'm sure he would have been long gone before 27. I always thought Roseanne didn't have a boyfriend and a son, she had two boys to look after, and she did because they loved each other so much. But it was a tragic love story and love doesn't pay the bills so after years of madness they split. But they did last longer than most of all their other pals, and when it was over Wullie went off the rails even more than usual. He was in self-destruct mode. Chris bumped into him one night and said he was full of vodka and Valium, and he was so stoned his eyes were like sharks' eyes, pure black.

The last time I saw Wullie I was walking into a shop to buy some beer and he was across the road. I looked over and saw he was well gone, could tell he had been drinking all day, so I just looked away and went into the shop. I had somewhere to go that night and I knew if he came with me it would just kick off. I was waiting for him to walk into the shop but he didn't and when I got outside he was gone. A week later I was in the pub waiting to get a beer when a guy walking past says, "sorry to hear about your pal, Wullie". I knew straight away he was dead and I was heartbroken that the last time I saw him I walked away. At his funeral a lot of people were looking at Roseann as if it was her fault he was gone. That pissed me off big time. All of these so-called family who didn't want anything to do with him, and here is this young girl who loved him and put up with him for years and just when she can't do it anymore Wullie goes and checks out, and they wanted to point the finger at her. Fuck off! That girl did more for my pal then his whole family put together. Anyway William died of a blood clot in his lung. No one was with him that night. All we know is he was in the pub, then went home with a carry out of vodka and beer, and that was the last anyone saw of him. Threatened by shadows at night and exposed in the light.

Wullie's funeral was a long sad day as all funerals are, but it was weird as much as it was heart breaking. I felt like a stranger at it. I didn't know many people who were there, maybe because I didn't know a lot of his family. Wullie wasn't close with many of his relatives; he was always with his girlfriend and son or his mum and his big brother, Ian, who I didn't have any time for. Ian was a drug addict and didn't help much in Wullie's mad young life. I mean, I'm no' saying he was a bad guy, I just think when life was upside down for Wullie, sitting getting high with his brother didn't help any. The day of the funeral I went up to the high-rise flats where Wullie's mum lived. I was asked to carry the coffin, and when I got there his mum asked me to go and make sure Ian was ready. When I went into his room he was so stoned he couldn't even get his suit on. At first I was mad, but then I started to think, 'this guy is burying his wee brother today, his heart is breaking just as much as mine and everyone has a weakness; drugs is his, so as much as drink will get me through this day, the drugs will get Ian through it'. So I helped him get ready. We had a wee talk about how much we loved Wullie and how we would make him proud today and give him a good send off.

When the undertaker showed up he asked who was carrying the coffin, could we step forward. He looked at us all, then looked at me and said "you will help me", and I'm thinking, 'with what?' We carried the coffin out the door to the lift and he said, "right, big man, me and you will take the coffin down in the lift. Everyone else carrying it, meet us at the bottom". So there I am, standing in the lift, with one of my best pals in his box, thinking this is fucked up. Never did I think this would happen to me. All those years sitting about joking and drinking and now I'm stuck in the lift with my mate, waiting to take him to his final resting place. As we got half way down the lift stopped and an old lady was about to get in. Her face was a picture; the poor old dear didn't know what to say, so I just went, "think you should maybe get the next one, hen," and she says, "I think you're right son".

When we got to the cemetery some of Wullie's family who, like I said, I had never seen before asked me nicely if I could step out and let one of his cousins carry the coffin and pointed to some guy I had never seen before, standing waiting to step in and take my place.

So I looked around at these strangers and said, "sorry boys but no". I could tell they weren't expecting that so I said, "look he was my best mate this past ten years and I never met any of yous over that time. Me and him were like brothers and I know if he was here he would tell me to stand my ground, and if any of yous knew him the way I did then you'd know I'm right".

No one said anything for about ten seconds, which is a long time when you're in the middle of strangers.

Then one of them went, "it's cool. I didn't know him that much. I'll step down," and I was thinking 'thank fuck for that; I don't need this shit, but I know I'm right. Wullie would have wanted me to carry him'.

After the funeral I didn't want to hang about. Like I said I didn't know many of them so I had a pint and talked to one of his cousins who asked me about Wullie and me being pals. He tuned out to be a good guy and said he hadn't seen Wullie because he'd moved down south.

I said, "look, I'm sorry but I had to carry my pal," and he said, "no you were right to say your bit". And as I finished my pint I said to his cousin, "it was good to meet you". And I didn't see his cousin again until a few years later when he popped up on crime watch.

Before I went I said goodbye to Roseann. It was like the end of a mad crazy chapter of our young lives. That day I walked to the pub just to clear my head and think about my pal, thinking how I would never see him again and have a beer, thinking how he would never grow old. It didn't seem fair, Wullie being gone. I always thought we would end up like two old pals meeting up for a beer and talking about the good old days, but as they say, some guys never grow old and Wullie was a rock'n'roll suicide. He's in the 27 club with some of the coolest people ever. Rest easy my friend, your madness is over now, and shine on you crazy diamond...

My other childhood pal, Brian Law died in 2018 at the age of 41, another guy who could play guitar like it was easy as walking in the park, but his life was always upside down. He liked to drink and take drugs but they didn't like him. He just wasn't built to drink. He got drunk too easy; after only a few cans he would have the hiccups. Round about 2010 he moved over to Ireland, got sober, and got a job working on a farm. It seemed his life was back on track. A few times over the years I would bump into him in Penilee and as much as I was happy to see him, I always thought he was better off back in Ireland, because Penilee was where all his demons lived. Brian was in a road accident and hurt his head but didn't get it checked out and a week later he came home for an aunt's funeral and died the next day. He had bleeding in the brain. He died in his old street where he grew up. I remember years ago me and Brian split up with our girlfriends at the same time, so because we were going through the same shit we went out drinking together for a few weeks, and the rest of our pals were fine with that because then they didn't have to listen to our bullshit; you know how guys with broken hearts can be.

So we took our wee broken hearts to the pub and I remember one day we were sitting talking, having a pint and a group of guys were playing pool beside us. So Brian says, "let's do a chip in for the jukebox, its four songs for a pound, so we put in 50p each. I told him to play The Stones but he puts the money in and bangs on his four songs. The first one comes on, and its 'Never Ever' by the girl group, All Saints. I'm like, "what the fuck are you playing that for," and he says, "it reminds me of my bird", and I'm like, "fuck off, the guys playing pool are looking over here and they're thinking you played it for me". And the other three songs were all love songs, too: The Eagles' Desperado, The Stones' Wild Horses and The Beatles' Something. It was a long four songs to sit through. I had to explain to him it was always a big deal to play the jukebox in the pub. First you had to make sure anyone who put money in got a song played by their favourite band, second, you had to really think about the first song you play because everyone in the pub will look round to see who is playing the jukebox and if you put on some shit love song you'll get a hard time from everyone on your way back to your table and third, the most important part about playing the jukebox is you have to find the songs that are the longest so you get your money's worth. On a Thursday night in the lounge we would all sit stoned and pick our favourite longest songs, like 'Midnight Rambler' and 'The End' by The Doors, and anything by Pink Floyd because all their songs are long. Brian took in every word and agreed that I had a good point, and I like to think he never ever played that song again.

The only problem about Brian being my pal was I could never get a bit of hash from any of the drug dealers in Penilee without getting a hard time from them about how Brian owed them tick. I was always like, "fuck all to do with me, I pay up front, I don't tick you so take it up with him," and they would always say, "we know but tell Brian I'm looking for him," and I would be thinking 'yeah you and about twenty other drug dealers, so good luck with that, pal'. It got so much of a pain in the ass with some of them saying shit like, "maybe I'll just take your money and you can go get it off your pal," and I'm like, "fuck off, its nothing to do with me so sell me a deal or I'll go elsewhere". And through time that's what I did. I would just get my old man to pick me up a bit and that way I got no hassle and more for my money. Like I said before, most of my pals couldn't sit about watching TV and drinking tea. They always wanted to get on it, so if they had money they wouldn't go and pay off their tick bill and be skint. No, they would just find another dealer to buy from, easy as that. Me and Brian didn't always see eye to eye but now he's gone I only have good memories about our time as pals. He was always up for a good time and could make everyone laugh. He just never worried about tomorrow. I asked Brian once many years ago what his favourite line from a song was? I was sure it would be a Beatles song as that was his favourite band, but he said to me it was Bob Dylan's song, 'don't think twice it's all right' and the line was... 'I gave her my heart but she wanted my soul'...

In 2018 I started to write this book not knowing if I could do it or not, and I didn't tell anyone apart from my daughter, Shawnay. She was the one who said if you put these stories onto paper people will read them, so I did a few pages and in January 2019 I took them round to Chris for him to have a look. I knew that even if he thought it was shit, Chris would still love it and be all proud of me, and tell me to keep going with it. But that day Chris was way too drunk to read anything so I didn't show him. Chris had been on the whisky for years and it was taking its toll on him. I mean, he was a strong guy and I always told him if I had drunk whisky like him I would have died years ago. But he was always OK, he never complained about hangovers or anything like that, and he was always ready to have a drink whenever any of his pals were. I think that's how you don't notice when your pal is drinking too much because I would drink with him and then I wouldn't drink for a few days, but one of the other guys would always be round at Fla's Bar. That day in January I went round I knew his life was upside down. We had lost Brian in November and Chris had lost his wee mum, Betty, in December.

Betty kept Chris busy. He did everything for his wee mum,

so when she passed away all of his pals knew we had to keep an eye on him, make sure our pal was OK. But he wasn't, because the house him and his mum had lived in was getting taken off him and he was too busy drinking to find anywhere to live. That day I went round we had a few beers and played some Pink Floyd and Rolling Stones songs just like old times. I asked him about the rest of the boys. He said Scott was down and I said what about Stuart? He said, "he was here last night but we fell out so he went home at 3am". I'm thinking that doesn't sound right but as the day went on I tried to talk to him about finding somewhere to live and he kept on saying, "it's OK, I'm taking care of it". I felt the more I went on about it, the more he was falling out with me, so I let it go and we sat drinking and talking about old times as we always did. Whenever I left Chris's house he always walked me to the gate; you know, we would have a few last words, then be on our way, and we did it that night. I told him I would be working for a few nights, then I'd be back round to see him. He said, "don't worry, I'll see you whenever, go and take care of your family".

I walked home that night and it was a full moon. I remember stopping to look at it with a sadness in my soul. I phoned Stuart the next day and he said he left that night because he couldn't watch his pal drink himself to death. I agreed with him and we said we would meet up on my days off to go round together. Three nights into my night shifts and Scott messaged me asking if I had seen or heard from Chris. I told him "no". He said Stuart had been round but got no answer at his door and his phone was off. The next morning

I got the news - Chris was in ICU, his liver was done in. All the years of whisky and too many good times as he would always say, had caught up with him. We think he had tried to stop drinking and hit the DTs and that's how no one could get hold of him. It breaks my heart to think another one of my pals died alone. The doctor turned off his life support machine on the 28th of January. God, I was fucking heartbroken. My pal of 29 years was gone, and I couldn't take it all in. None of his pals could. We knew he wouldn't live to be an old man, and some even said he wouldn't last long after losing his wee mum, but seven weeks! No one saw that coming, except maybe Chris - who knows?

When you lose your pal all the old memories come flooding back and that's the hard part; you walk about like a ghost, just lost. Chris's brother, Mick, gave us the keys to Chris's house so we could get a keepsake each. That was hard. I got round to his house first and stood at the gate in the dark, alone. It was weird after all the years standing there with him and now it was just me. When the rest of the boys showed we all walked in apart from Scott. I looked back and he was just standing at the gate looking up at the bedroom window. I had to go to him and walk in the door with him. In the bedroom we all stood looking around talking about all the good times. Me and Stuart were making jokes and laughing with the boys but it was hard for us all to be there and Chris wasn't. So we all got a keepsake and left. I took an out of date can of beer he had in his room since 2002, by the look on Scott's face the only thing he wanted was to get out. It was all too much for him, too many memories.

I told Scott to take a breath, take his time and have a look around the house. I didn't want him to just rush off and not get anything, but on the other hand I could see how he was feeling. Walking about our dead pal's house didn't feel right. It didn't feel real standing in his room thinking about all the years gone by, all the dark cold winter nights and all the hot summer days, just us pals, drinking and smoking and listening to music with not a care in the world, and now the ring master, the glue of the gang, was gone. It was like a bad dream. I went downstairs into his wee mum's living room. I just stood there in the empty room and thought about all the times over the years I had popped in to see his mum for a chat before going up the stairs for a beer. I kept thinking how many more empty rooms am I going to stand in thinking of the past, just standing there with a broken heart.

As the boys were getting ready to go I had one last look around. I went into the kitchen it was empty like most of the house because his brothers had only a short amount of time to get it empty for the housing to take it back. As I looked around the empty kitchen I opened a cupboard door and looked in. I couldn't believe what I found. It was a shot glass I got him in 1999 when I was on holiday in Vegas. You know the wee shit gifts we get each other on holiday - well this was one of them. It had his name on it and a picture of the Vegas strip. I couldn't believe after all these years he still had it and the funny thing is at the time I got myself one, too, and I still had that one as well. I stood in that empty kitchen looking at this wee shot glass thinking how time really does go by way too fast. I mean, I still remember going into the hotel shop to buy him that gift. I remember giving it to him and we both had a shot of whisky out of them and talked about my holiday to America. I couldn't take it all in. That was twenty years ago but it only felt like two years ago.

Looking in that empty house in the empty kitchen at that wee glass was the moment I realised my pal of thirty years was gone. Time had caught up with us. We weren't kids anymore, the party was over, last orders at the bar. Now I like to think back to when we were young and skint, running about trying to find £8 to get a bit of hash or maybe £10 so we could get some beers, too. It felt now like we didn't have a care in the world, but we probably did and I just can't remember. But what I do remember is all the nights it was just me and Fla before all the rest of the guys come along, before any girlfriends, it was just me and him smoking dope in his room and he had the best record collection ever, and it was him who got me into music. My love for The Rolling Stones still to this day is because of Fla. Whenever we were at a party and I would be going on about The Stones being the best band in the world he would always say to whoever I was talking to, "sorry, that's my fault, I made him Stones mad". Back then when we were struggling for cash a guy in the pub who worked in a whisky factory would sell us three bottles in a bag for £10 - the deal was you pick a bag, you couldn't pick the bottles. It was like the best game ever. I would let Fla pick a bag, then we would have a look to see what we got and you always got maybe two good bottles and one shit one, but once everyone had a bag we would always hold up the shit one and see if anyone wanted a swap. It was like a game show.

I would hold it up and say, "I have a bottle of spice rum, who wants it? Anyone? Maybe someone's wife's birthday soon?"

Then someone would go, "I'll swap you it for a bottle of martini".

.... "fuck off keep your martini, pal".

But two good bottles and one shit bottle was good for £10. We would always head back to his with our carry out and a bit of hash to chill and listen to music. I will miss how Fla would shout out loud the word "boring" when someone was talking a lot of shit. It was so embarrassing. We would walk into the pub and some guy who I had worked with in the past would say "hi" and try to tell me about his new house and how he got a good deal on it and Fla would belt out "boring!!" Then he'd just take a drink of his pint and the poor guy would be speechless. I miss my pal every day and I am forever grateful to Fla for getting me into so many great bands because we all know the songs help us get through life, good times or bad times. Goodbye, Fla. Take it easy mate and as you would always say, "you can check out any time you like, but you can never leave!"

Big Shug Boyle went downhill a few years after my dad passed away. His lungs were in a bad way with all the years of smoking but whenever my brother Gerry was up the road for a visit Shug would always make it to the pub for a drink. It was like old times. If I went in for a pint anyone who was in would just say, "alright? How's things?" but because Gerry and Shug came in and had no' been in for a long time, everyone would head over and sit in the corner. So it would be me, my brother Gerry, Shug, Rab Fraser, Pat Fla, Mick Boyle and Rab Donnelly, and this was the end of the gang, but it was just like old times and I loved it. Big Shug died with the swine flu; he fought it as best he could but his lungs couldn't take it. I missed saying goodbye to him by a few minutes. He got taken into the hospital where I worked and asked his sister to go find Joe. "Bring him up here. He'll make sure I get some good grub." But I was just away home from work when she came to look for me, and he passed away the next day. His wife Sandra told me he seemed really stressed just before he went, moving about the bed, and she took his hand and told him, "Shug, I'll be OK. If it's time to go, then just go. I love you," and he stopped moving about, his breathing slowed down and he passed away. Another one of my pals now behind the sun way too soon. I always think of Shug when I'm sitting round an open fire having a drink, the simple things in life.

In 2018 I had my last ever drink with Mick Boyle. He had been through the wars with throat cancer again. All the years of drinking and smoking had taken its toll on him, but let's face it, I don't think any of these guys had regrets about it; they were never going to sit in the house, drink tea and watch the TV. No, they knew the life they had chosen and it was fun while it lasted. Mick was a walking miracle; the doctors were wanting him to go to meet other doctors to show them this guy who was never mind still alive, but was still drinking alcohol and smoking. They couldn't believe he could talk because of how much of his throat they had taken away but there he was, sitting in the pub having a beer and talking to me. You could hear his voice struggling and he told me he couldn't get food down but he was definitely going to make it to the Argosy for a beer. He could only drink about two or three pints at the most, but it kept him busy, gave him something to live for I suppose. One day in 2018 I had a beer with him and we talked and laughed about old times and when he was going home he said to me," goodbye Joe, I'll see you on the other side, pal," and that was the last time I ever saw him. He passed away the same day as Chris Fla's mum, Betty, and his funeral was on the same day, too, which made it hard for me to be there for Chris, then leave him to go to Mick's. But I had to. Mick had been my pal for 25 years. He was one of my first pals in the pub and always got me a pint when I was young and skint, or gave me a puff on a joint like most of my dad's pals did.

It's a quiet corner now, just me, Rab and Pat Fla still haunting it. Big Gerry Law went off the radar a few years ago. I'm told he goes drinking in the town from time to time, but I have no' seen him in years; maybe one day - I hope so. I miss Big Gerry. Him and all the boys made me the man I am today. They let a fifteen year old kid into the gang and I will never forget that, and thanks to them I have some good memories of growing up in a pub, instead of running about the streets off my face. You see, most people thought that my dad taking me to the pub at fifteen was bad but he taught me how to take my time with the drink; there was no rush to get drunk. He would point out to me how fucked up some guy was and say, "do you want to be like that," and all the guys gave me tips on growing up and staying out of trouble. The one thing all the boys agreed with was you don't want to do jail time.

Looking back now in my forties and thinking about all the

guys I was pals with that are now gone, I think to myself 'is this how a soldier feels when he goes to war and is the only guy to make back out of the jungle?' I don't want anyone to feel sorry for me and all that 'poor me' shit. No, I know how lucky I am. I was a fifteen year old kid who got into this cool gang, and they made me the man I am today. And they might all be gone but their memories live on in all the good times

Chris and me were in the Pines pub having a beer or two, and a family were sat at the next table to us and were talking about things that happen to everyone in life, like when you pull a green crisp out of the bag of crisps and you're no' sure whether to eat it, or how everyone had an uncle who stole your nose, and I said to Chris, "that's fuck all, our uncle tried to steal your virginity" and the family asked if they could move tables. I would stay at Chris's house a lot when we were young, we all did, but when he was ready to sleep he would always light a cigarette and it would piss me off. I was the only guy who didn't smoke so I was always on at my pals to give it up. So one night I wake up and Chris's blanket he is sleeping under is up in flames. I jumped up and shook him to get out of the bed. Then I turned round, grabbed a can of beer, opened it, turned back to put out the fire with it and Chris, who is still asleep, not knowing what's going on, has sat up, got a cigarette and is trying to get a light off the flames. I swear I had to drag him out the bed.

Every Thursday back in the day Helen, the barmaid, would work up in the lounge in the Argosy. It was never busy, just me, Chris, my dad and our uncle Joe who would pop down now and again for a quiet pint. Joe was class. He was so funny, like if he stood up he would go, "fuck me, I'm stiffer than a honeymooner's prick," or if my dad was talking to him about something from years back he would say, "yeah, it's like baking a cake in the oven", and I would ask what that had got to do with it and he would say, "I forgot all about it". At the end of the night just before last orders my dad and Joe would head home and me and Chris would take a seat at the bar for our last beer. Helen, the barmaid, would pour our pints, then cash up the till. But when she stood at the till she had her back to us so me and Chris would talk to her to distract her. "Been busy tonight, Helen?" She would answer back but never look round because she was busy counting the till, so as we chatted we would also help ourselves to another beer. We would drink more beer in the twenty minutes it took her to cash up then we had drunk all night. We did this for weeks. Then one night she poured our last pints of the night and pulled down the shutters - some fucker had stuck us in. Helen had a husband who drank in the pub, Big Tam. He had been in an accident at work - a crane hit him on the head in Arrow's shipyard - so his nickname was Arrow Head. He took a fit at the front of the pub doors and everyone was too busy watching Celtic play so I was the only guy who went over to him. All I could think to do was to hold him still so he didn't choke or hurt himself. After he came to he got me a beer and a half of whisky and so did the manager of the pub. My old man was well pissed off that he didn't help.

'Still Game' is a TV programme in Scotland and everyone loves it in Glasgow. All the guys in the pub would talk about it every week and the week Chris passed away they showed the last ever episode and the song at the end of the last show was Bob Dylan's 'don't think twice it's alright'. I couldn't believe it! The show that we all loved was ending the same week as I was saying goodbye to Chris and the song we all played in the pub, it was the perfect goodbye to all my pals. Every time I watch Still Game it's like spending time with old pals. It's like I'm back sitting in the pub. All the old guys who didn't want to grow up.

I'm walkin' down that long, lonesome road, babe Where I'm bound, I can't tell But goodbye's too good a word, gal So I'll just say fare thee well

On the 25th of October 2021 I just got home from a four day drinking holiday in Spain. I was knackered, and in need of a curry and more beer when my daughter told me at the door that gran had phoned and she said to tell you that Gerry Law had died. I sat in the hall on the stairs thinking a million things at the same time; all the memories came flooding back. I hadn't seen Gerry in years - he had gone off the radar years back - but it was still sad to hear of his passing. A few days went by and word round the camp fire was that he had died of cancer, and that when he was told he had it he refused any treatment. That last bit, I don't know if it's true but it sounds like Gerry. He would have just said, "if it's time then it's time, I don't need anyone cleaning my ass". Years ago me, my dad and Gerry were talking about being eighteen again, you know, getting a second chance to live your life over again, and my old man was all for it. He said he would love another bite at the cherry, but Gerry was like, fuck that! This one has been long enough," and I didn't get a say because I was still young at the time.

Everyone was asking each other if anyone knew when his funeral was and no one seemed to know. I kept thinking that maybe there won't be one. Maybe if Gerry knew he was checking out he could have one last 'fuck you everyone, no cunt's getting any steak pie from me". Turns out I was right. He didn't have anything. He would leave this life the same way as John Lennon and David Bowie did, with no fuss. I like that he did that. I was happy with waiting a few weeks, then going on a hunt to find where he was laid to rest and I knew it was in the same cemetery as my old man. So two old pals back together and thinking about it, if he had a funeral most of the cunts who would have shown up would have been fucking hypocrites, doing their noisy eyes full of tears - yeah more like full of shit cunts who didn't like him or hadn't seen him in twenty years, but still want to stand there and give it the 'poor me, I lost someone' thing. Fuck off!

That same week the Argosy had got done up and had reopened so a few days later that week I went for a pint. I sat in the same corner as always, had a look around the new pub and had a drink to Gerry - one of the last of the Compost Corner gang. Most of them are gone now, blown and scattered like autumn leaves. Maybe only two or three of them still alive and drinking in the pub are Pat Fla, Mick Reid and Rab Fraser (who is still barred). But as I was sitting enjoying my beer thinking about Gerry a song came on the jukebox; it was The Verve's 'Sonnet' from 1997. You know how a song can take you back in time - well that song hit me like I had been run over by a fucking DeLorean. I went right back to the good old days when the corner was jumping with ten guys squeezed around a table meant for four, and you couldn't see anyone for the cloud of smoke. I couldn't shake it off sitting there now, alone, thinking if I only I had known back then that in twenty six years I would be the last guy at the party, that guy who won't take a hint and fuck off home.

I will miss big Gerry just as I miss the rest of the guys. I was his pal's son, and then in time, his pal, too. We had some good days together drinking, and I was proud to be sitting with guys like Gerry and Rab because I was a young kid and could see guys older than me trying to be friends with them and they didn't get let into the gang. But there I was drinking and smoking with not a care in the world. To be fair most of it is a blur what with all the hash we were smoking. We would get a bag of grass and mix it with hash - 'joint cocktails' I called them - and on a Sunday we would puff them all day long, washing them down with cold beer, and we would get so stoned that it seemed hard work just to go home, I'm no' kidding! A few days later you would go in for a beer and Gerry would say, "I was so stoned on Sunday I didn't know how to say I'm heading off," and someone like Mick Boyle would say, "yeah, I was the same, I missed my dinner and the wife was pissed off at me". Everyone has a weakness and hash was Gerry's. He lived to get stoned. He hated the taste of alcohol and got bad hangovers with it so once he found hash he was done with getting pissed. He told me he would smoke hash in his flat till he couldn't move and thinking back now, he must have spent thousands on hash over the years. Goodbye Gerry, and if you need a friend I'm sailing right behind.

173

So now most of the gang are all but gone, only a few kicking about in their old age like Rab Fraser. He is the last of that gang. He's in his late sixties but in his head and heart he still feels 25. He is on and off the drink these days, so much that I'm scared to phone him to go for a beer because I will put him back on it again. He is just one of those guys who can't go for a few pints. No, once he gets a few he's back on the runaway train - alcoholic I think it's called. The only thing that stops Rab from drinking too much now is old age and the fact that when he is drinking, he is downing over a litre of vodka a day, easy; but sober or drunk Rab hasn't changed one bit, he still has the heart of a lion. Like I said before, most of these guys would have lived to a good age if it wasn't for their life style. But Rab never moans about being old and I don't think he has many regrets considering the life he has had. I mean, he's spent the best part of it in the jail, he's been stabbed, slashed and hit over the head with more beer bottles than I have drunk, but that to him was fuck all. He didn't lose when it came to fighting, and he wasn't a bully. No, he would beat the shit out of a bully, and any time I saw him get into a fight he would always ask the guy, "are you sure you want to do this," every time. And the poor guy would say "yes," then a few minutes later wished he had said "no".

Rab never boasted about being hard or being a good fighter, he was just wanting to get a drink with his pals, unlike most guys who would sit and try and impress you about their life, but really they were boring you to death with it. Rab wasn't like that. I mean, a guy once told me that Rab's first wife was killed by a shotgun, and I was like, no way! He had never said.

And then one day I was sitting drinking with him and I asked him, "what happened to your first wife?"

Rab stared at me for a few seconds like he always did and in that few seconds you didn't know which way this was going to go. Then he said, "who told you I had been married before, boy?"

I said, "word around the camp fire is that she was killed".

He burst out laughing and said, "word around the camp fire - I like that one," and then he said, "yeah I was married before and we split and I met Peter" (his second wife – real name, Jackie). He said, "I was in the jail when I got a phone call from my old mum, and she told me 'your ex has been killed - her new husband has shot her' and I said 'so' and my old mum said, 'well I wanted you to know'".

He said, "she got married to some mad fucker after she split from me".

And I'm thinking, 'what madder than you?'

He continued, "he got into a fight, came home to get his shotgun to go and deal with the guys he was fighting with, but they showed up at his door with a team of guys. So my ex-wife stood in front of the door to try and stop him from going out and shooting them, and in the middle of all the shouting get out the fucking way, the gun went off and killed the poor woman instantly".

I was like, "fucking hell, Rab cunts in here want to bore me to death with stories about their new houses or their kids and you have a story like that, and don't tell me".

He said, "it was a long time ago, boy, a long time ago".

Rab was a big strong guy but he didn't go to the gym or anything like that. he was just naturally strong; one of them lucky cunts, unlike me. I would always tell him how lucky he was to be that strong and he would say, "what are you talking about, boy". He had hands like shovels and his arms were like Popeye's, but he didn't have one tattoo.

I would always say, "what a waste of an arm".

Then, one day I told him if he went with me for a tattoo I would pay for it, and he says, "I wouldn't know what to get".

I said, "if I'm paying you're getting a wee girl dog with a pink ribbon on its head".

And he was like, "what's the big deal with my arms anyway".

I'm like, "look at the size of them, and you don't lift weights. If I went to the gym for two years and lifted heavy weights my arms would still look like two knots on a flea's dick".

Rab was one of the few who worked. He was a mechanic with his brothers. He drank in the town, then made his way to the Argosy before going home. The pubs he drank in were rough shitholes but he knew everyone and everyone knew him. After a few drinks in the town he would hit the Argosy, get a round in and sit down. I would ask him, "where have you been?" and he would tell me about all the pubs, and he went on about the Clyde Inn, this wee pub on the Paisley Road, just before you turn into the town. He loved it in there, so one night me and my old man says let's go and meet him in the Clyde Inn. We jumped on a bus and when we walked in there he was at the bar being loud as ever. When he saw us he went nuts; I'm telling you it was like you'd think we had bumped into him in Australia and had no' seen him for years instead of just meeting him five minutes up the road. He introduced us to all the guys in the pub who were then getting us a drink, and me and my dad were thinking, 'so far, so good'. We sat at a table in the corner of the pub and Rab was buzzing to see us. He was like, "we'll have a few then, get a taxi to the Argosy - make a night of it," and we were fine with that. And as the night was rolling along I noticed a drunk guy asleep at the next table and his suit jacket was hanging off him because he was hanging off the chair. But I wasn't worried about him falling off the chair.

What was worrying me was the gun sticking out of his suit jacket, so I said to Rab, "what's the story with the guy at the next table?"

Rab looked and said, "he's just split from his wife and he's not taking it to good".

I said, "you couldn't tell with that gun sticking out of his suit jacket,"

Rab looked over, shouted on the barmaid, who came over and covered the gun back up with his jacket, like, job done.

I looked at my old man and said, "taxi?"

A few days later I was telling Gerry about our night out and he said, "yeah I went up there last year and a guy who knew Rab offered me a line, and when I went into the toilet there were three lines out, and I was thinking that's all for me then and snorted the lot. Only afterwards the guy says, 'you were only meant to take one', so I bought a few drinks and fucked off".

We didn't go to many other pubs, we stuck to the Argosy and only went to others a handful of times, like when John Bone-eye got married. Me, my dad, Gerry, Rab and Shug Boyle all went to the night-time party. I loved it, going to a party with them, but they all hated being away from the pub. When we walked into the wedding party we joined a queue to meet and congratulate the new couple.

As we were standing in the queue Rab turned to me and said, "I've forgotten his wife's name, what is it again?"

I said, "it's Linda," and he said, "cheers".

So we get to the front of the queue and Rab says, "Linda, you look amazing," and goes to give her a kiss when the new bride says, "who the fuck is Linda, I'm Margaret".

Well Rab stops, says to Linda, I mean Margaret, "sorry, hen. Give me a second," and turns round to me and says, "funny cunt, we'll talk about this later".

Well, I couldn't move for laughing. He turned back, says "sorry" and took off for the bar. My dad was at the bar and told me that Rab came up and said "I'm buying everyone a drink apart from your fucking boy".

You know, you could always count on Rab for a good time. As soon as you went in for a pint and Rab was in you knew this was going to get messy, but I like messy. You remember when you got into trouble when you were a kid and your mum would be talking to some neighbour and she would say, "he's no' a bad lad, he's just got in with the wrong crowd" - well, I was the wrong crowd. I was the first to smoke or drink and take drugs out of all my pals in Pollok, and when I moved to Penilee I got all my new pals who maybe liked a bit of hash into Es and LSD. I think every guy in the pub was the same as me - we were the wrong crowd, and that's why it worked. Two odds make an even, and I knew hundreds of guys who like my dad, Gerry and Rab, but I also knew hundreds who didn't like them. But they didn't give a fuck who didn't like them because they didn't have the balls to say it to their face and didn't drink in the Argosy. Anyway most of the haters were just jealous cunts. Rab is the last of the Mohicans in his sixties still getting drunk and stoned like he's in The Stones, Glasgow's own Keith Richards, and if I was to describe him he is just like Oliver Reed - he is his spit, even the 'tash, and always drunk and kissing you, and calling everyone darling, and when he wanted a hug you had no choice in the matter.

Every one of the guys I talked about in this book are now gone and most of them, I feel, have left no trace of ever having been alive. I mean, out of my three pals my own age, only Brian Law has a headstone; Wullie and Chris don't, so I have nowhere to pay my respects to them on a birthday or anniversary. And I know you don't need a headstone to be remembered; I can do that by just going for a beer or maybe watching their favourite films on their birthdays and that, but as I tell this story it's like it could have all been a dream because all these guys are just my memories. Maybe that's why I decided to do this book, because once I'm gone there would be no story. I know when I sit in the Argosy now you would never have known these guys had been and gone. Sometimes I could be in the pub now, having a beer, looking over at a table where the drug dealers used to sell their gear and it has three old ladies sitting at it sharing a bottle of wine and it's no'

Eldorado. But maybe it's just as well, because I couldn't do it all now, I'm too old, or I don't want to get too old, too fast, if that makes sense. I respect alcohol now; I stick with beer and maybe a glass of wine. I don't bust a bottle of Jack Daniel's now and drink it till it's done. No, I take my time. As I said before, or my old man did, there's no hurry in getting drunk, take your time, you will always get there in the end. I loved Jack Daniel's back in the day and maybe that's why I can't handle it all now - too many good times. I've spent all my beer tokens in life and Jack is not the whisky you fuck with - it's too cool to be messed around with. But I was using it like a junkie using junk. I was drinking it no' to have a good time, but to just get on with my day - you know, a wee Jack before we head out, or a wee Jack to sort out this hangover - stuff like that. But all the guys lived the same way. We just each had a different drink, and I know what you're thinking. Why didn't I just stop drinking? Because, as my brother Gerry always said, to me drinking non-alcoholic beer is like licking your sister's fanny - it tastes the same but you know there's something no' right about it. But if you're going to be a hard drinker, than you drink hard - simple as that. Accept the path you choose in life and get on with it. and like most guys in the pub that's what they did. They were big enough and ugly enough to know what they were doing; only problem was I wasn't, I was just a kid and had no idea about what was ahead for me for the next thirty years. But if I was to be honest, if I got offered now to do it all again I would do it faster than a New York minute. How good it would be to get another got at my drunken youth - wild horses couldn't drag me away.

Sex, drugs and signing the dole

DON'T LET THE SAME DOG BITE YOU TWICE.

CHAPTER 6

This is the Strangest Life
I Have Ever Known..

Times change as you get older and you have to just go with it, ride the wave, because if you stop and get off the bus, the world won't hang around waiting on you, and I think that's why some of us hate getting old. We make the mistake of thinking the world is in a bad way because it didn't wait on us. That's when you find yourself saying daft shit like, 'in my day we couldn't afford that' and 'we only had this'. That's when you should have a word with yourself. But it's OK if you say it now and then. Getting old happens to the best of us. I do it when I sit in the pub and watch the young team downing shots till they can't tell if it's New York or New Year. It's madness! I don't get it at all, and the first thing I tell my own kids is, 'don't think the more alcohol you drink the better time you have' but I suppose everyone needs to learn the hard way.

Another thing is, you can forget how bad you were when you were young. I mean, we were that bad, I don't think I want to remember. If you were to see some of us sitting in the pub back in the day we would have looked OK I'm sure, but we were far from it. Me and Brian were barred out of all the off sales shops for stealing drink and fags - that's cigarettes, just in case you're thinking, my God they were kidnapping homosexuals! It was so easy. The staff were behind the counter in a cage for their own safety and they would pass the drink through to you. The staff were behind the counter in a cage for their own safety and they would pass the drink through to you. What we would do was go into the shop and always get a bottle of Jack Daniel's, six cans of beer and twenty fags and then ask for whatever was furthest away from the counter. You would say, "oh, and give us 2 packets of salt and vinegar crisps, please," and as soon as they got to the faraway item we were off out the door and halfway down the street before they knew what had happened. Most of the time the staff would give chase but not for too long because they couldn't leave the shop empty, or by the time they got back there would have been nothing left. The first time we did it we got back to my house all out of breath. I poured us a Jack and Brian said, "mate, it always tastes better when it's free".

Brian was a good thief, there was no getting away from it - he knew how to steal and he had the balls to do it. He was the only one of us to do a bit of time, He would act daft, but the stuff he would come up with was pure class. Like the time he moved in with his girlfriend. He told me he loved staying with her but her mum showed up every day and she hated him.

He said, "I'm OK with that because she is a total cunt".

I said, "what are you going to do?"

He said, "I don't know. I'm still thinking about it". Then about a week later we were having a drink and I asked him how things with the old mother-in-law were going and he said, "all good, mate. I found out that she's terrified of spiders so I went straight to the pet shop and bought the biggest tarantula they had. Job done, mate".

See as you get older you don't think like that anymore. You just surrender to it, put up with it anything - for a quiet life. Sometimes things happen to me and I think for a second, 'right what would Chris do about this or Wullie'? Then I think what they would really do or say, and just 'fuck that. I might get the jail' and as I always told my pals, I'm too pretty for prison. Chris always said if you went to jail they would play cards for your wee ass, mate. Fuck that. Time to keep my nose clean because he who sticks his nose in a beehive will get more than a nose full of honey, as they say. Nope there is no getting away from it. We all get old in the end. We all become just like our parents, worried about our kids, and think 'why are they not home yet - the street lights are on? Peter Kay says you know you're turning into your dad when you find a stick and keep it for stirring paint. Well, I noticed I was turning into my old man when I finished my Jack and Coke and shook the empty glass over my pint like it was a salt shaker, thinking I needed to get that last wee drop of whisky out.

Nowadays guys go to the pub for a night out with the girlfriend, but back in the day that didn't happen. The pub back then was a man's place, to get away from the wife and get drunk, and talk about how you just missed out on playing for Celtic or Rangers because you had to get married, and most of the guys talking this shit couldn't kick their own ass. They would go on and on about it, week in and week out. If busting a guy's ears was a crime most of those cunts would have got life. You know the ones I'm talking about - they give it all the 'if only I'd done this' shit. I would just cut them off and say, "look, ifs don't come into it; if my aunty had nuts she would be my uncle," or "here's 10p; go away and phone some cunt who gives a fuck". When I first went into the pub it did have a few females in it as regulars. I got on with them all because I was a young kid so they'd give me a few beers and told me, "don't grow up like your dad and his pals". The girls sat up at the other end of the bar and big Rab called it 'Slutsville. Most of the girls could drink you under the table and some of them could fight just as good as some of the guys. My dad and his pals didn't have anything good to say about them because men like them came from a time when a women should be at home making dinner like their mums did for their dad. So they would want to fuck them, but didn't want to sit with them. The guys would say things like, "a woman is like a monkey, they don't let go of one branch till they get a good grip on the next one," and the nicknames they gave them said it all – 'Wee Vodka Head' and 'Luscious Linda'.

My dad said to me one day, "some of girls might be cows but they're good cows". I told him I didn't know the difference from a cow and a good cow and he said, "a good cow will let you fuck her, and in the morning she will maybe give you a few pounds to get a few beers". At 15 years old I was telling my pals that we needed to find ourselves a good cow and live happily ever after. As I said, some of the birds could fight, and everyone knew not to mess with them. Big Carolina was one of the best fighters out of them I had seen, and she was a really good looking bird. If you were a stranger sitting having a wee beer you might look at her and think 'I'd give her one' and then the next thing she is hitting someone with a pint glass, and she did that quite a few times over the years. Some of these girls smoked dope, drank and stayed out all weekend, never up or down. The guys would go home with them, then sit and joke about it the next day, like, "how did you get on last night," and my dad would say, "she asked me to kiss her somewhere wet and smelly so I took her to Greenock," or "when I got up in the morning I was putting my working boots on the wrong way round and she says' those boots are on the wrong feet' and I said 'I know they should be on yours'". The guys loved all the dirty talk. I was lost; maybe too young to take it all in, but looking back I know they were just a lost generation. My dad would always say they don't want shopping bags, they all want fucking handbags and are too busy going out to look after their kids. It was all just the times changing, and these guys didn't know how to take it all in. The last of the Mohicans, a lost generation of the sixties, the good old days.

Still, to this day, some of the girls from the pub are my pals and they are still going strong, what with females living longer than males it's not hard. One of my best pals from the pub is Wee Bunty; she's been my drinking buddy for thirty years. Always looking out for everyone, she is a good friend to have by your side. She's like the sister I never had and it's always good to bump into her. It's like the old gang getting back together. And my other girl pal for years is Big Linda. I'm so happy to call her a pal because no one wants to be on the wrong side of Linda. She doesn't take any shit. Big Rab is best pals with Linda and is always taking the piss with her, and he is a braver man than me. Linda's mum, Helen, was the first woman in the pub to look out for me. Helen was always happy, nothing ever got her down and if she was to sit and sing she sounded like Rod Stewart. It was unreal how much she sounded like him. None of the boys liked Rod that much but I did, so when Helen got up and sang I was only joking I loved it. She was amazing. I can still see and hear it to this day from all those years ago.

Back when my dad was a boy if someone's mum was single it was only because she was a widow, not because she was wanting more out of life, like a good career or a new car, and maybe a bit of me-time like two weeks in Ibiza with some guy she doesn't know hanging about like a dug way a burst baw trying to get into your city slickers. No, back in the day if you were a women life was shit, but fucking tough. You just had to get on with it, take the kids to school, and try and feed a family of about ten with no fucking money. I would sit in the pub and think to myself, no wonder the females got out; they must have been fed up to fuck, and if you listen to The Rolling Stones song, 'Mother's Little Helpers' that's what they are singing about - young girls so fed up they need pills just to get through the day. The good thing was I had a front row seat watching this rebellion. The pub would be full of girls looking to have a good time and the boys would be going nuts, saying they're taking over like it was the SS coming in for a drink. One night the lounge had a male stripper on and the bar was full of a lot of unhappy husbands and boyfriends. I was told that this big good looking guy come out the gents toilet, naked, holding just a small sheet. Just thinking back then, all the smoke in the pub it must have looked like stars in their eyes. We could hear them going nuts from downstairs, right, so this dude is going round all the girls and putting the sheet over their head so they can get a wee peek at the goods, but he gets about three rows in, puts it over some girl's head, then just hangs about looking like he is trying to work out algebra. So someone pulls the sheet away and the girl is sucking his cock. All the girls think this is so funny, and just another crazy night, all just the sort of stuff that happens on a girls night shit. Except one wee sneaky cow who makes her way down to the bar to tell the girl's husband, and yeah, he went fucking nuts. I was down the back of the pub playing pool when I got told to go and stop one of the boys from killing the stripper. Me and a few guys got hold of the husband at the door, while a few other guys put the stripper out of the fire exit and into a taxi. The boys had hold of the husband while I tried to talk to him. I gave it the old 'take it easy, you don't want to get the jail' and then he said it - the line I will never forget as long as I live - he said, "it's no' that, Joe. It's just …she doesn't even suck my dick.

This was the new world and the boys couldn't keep up. There was a guy who sat near us, Big Tam. He didn't have a wife or many pals but one night in the pub a girl half his age sat down with a drink and Tam got talking to her. So as the night rolled on she says, "let's get a carry out and got back to your flat. Tam must have been thinking he had won the lottery. How could he get so lucky - this young bird wants to go back to his wee shithole of a flat, so Tam takes her in, puts the two bars on the electric fire, gets the best of the sixties hit cassette tape on, and it's party time. The girl asks him if he's ever taken an ecstasy pill. Tam says, "no, hen, why?" She tells him it makes the sex one hundred times better. He takes the pills, washing then down with a large whisky and then wakes up in the morning to an empty flat, and I mean empty! She and whoever she was working with took the lot; the only thing they didn't get was the bed the poor big cunt was sleeping on, but the girl was right - he did get fucked.

All these guys were lost in a new generation. They grew up watching their mums running about after their dads and now couldn't work out why their wives weren't doing the same. It wasn't really their own fault they were such bad husbands - they just didn't know any better. At that time, around about the middle eighties, they all lost their jobs, hit the drink because they had fuck all to do, then they lost their families. They didn't know what had hit them all, poor lost souls! In the early nineties most guys in their forties and fifties were back staying with their parents and it didn't seem strange because they were all doing it. Sometimes you would see a guy in the pub look at his watch and go, "shit, I'm late for my tea, my mum will be going mad," then run out the door to mother. One day I was on the bus going to work when at a stop a mother and her 50 year old son got on.

The old mother couldn't find her bus pass and the driver said, "it's OK, take your time, hen," but her son wasn't happy and said, "hurry up and move mum, you're holding up the bus".

And the old dear looks at him and says, "you should hurry up and move out, you're holding up my life".

Everyone these days is fed up with life because they spend so much time on Facebook and Instagram, trying to make out all is fine, giving it the 'oh look at me' bullshit, just a wee reminder of me and my man having a ball in New York, when in fact it's May and she's no' seen him since New Year, never mind New York. But are they the fools, or is it us who follow this shit and like it? It's hard work these days for the young team to get drunk and still look good at 3am in some shit night club, when you're pal wants to get a picture of you in the toilets and you only went in for a shit. Fuck that! Twenty years ago people would think you were doing good because you could afford a two week holiday to Spain. Back then you didn't need to worry about how you looked because no cunt had a camera in your face every time you took a drink. Back then you could go for a beer without your girlfriend because she didn't want to go because the pub was a shithole she wouldn't be seen dead in. Then a few years back they made all the pubs look nice and do shit like food and cocktails, so now it costs you double if you want to go to the pub, well more than double because she is on the cocktails at about £7 a drink. But times change. Like I said, going on holiday was easy then. Now it's all six days in Las Vegas and eight days in Mexico; work yourself to death for a holiday. My first holiday abroad was a wee shit B&B in Greece, but It was amazing because the sun was out, we had a pool, and a pint of beer was only 70p. I mean, you would get a phone card, find a phone box, phone the pub, ask if Arthur Reavey was in and then tell your dad how much it was for a beer. Never mind all that 'how's the hotel and the food' - you were too busy telling your pals 'it's only 70p for a fucking beer, yeah mate I'm moving over here next year'.

Not a lot of guys in the pub went on holiday back then. One guy, Frank, whose nickname was 'Mother' because he was always telling us he was going to see mother today, in her old folks home.

Well, he was somewhere in Spain in a market and asked a young girl, "how much for this, hen," and she says, "you're from Glasgow, aren't you?"

"Yes," says Frank, "how did you know? Is it my broad Scottish accent?"

"No," said the wee girl, "it's that Farmfoods' bag you have".

You know when you ask someone, "how was your holiday," even though you don't care, but they bore the ass off you about it, well, the best answer I ever heard was when I overheard two old girls talking and one asked the other, "how was your holiday?" and her pal says, "you know it was so good I didn't need my cardigan the whole holiday". I told my dad and his pals that, thinking it was a funny story and they all looked at each other and Gerry said, "that sounds like a good holiday to me".

It's good going on holiday when you're just at the beginning of a relationship. You know what's it's like when you first meet a girl, all you want to do is eat her, and for the rest of your life you wished you fucking had, but when you first get together you have to be Mr Nice Guy.

Like if she falls walking up the stairs with the shopping you go, "oh, what you like, you're so silly, just as well you're pretty,"

then a year down the line if she falls you go, "oh for fuck sake, you silly cunt, you better have no' bust any of my cans of beer".

Or you get a takeaway and she didn't get any chips for herself, but asks you for some of yours you're like, "yeah, here - have them all,"

then a year later it's "if you wanted chips you should have got some, and maybe it's just as well you didn't get any,"

and then she will say, "do you think I'm fat?

I'm no' saying you're fat, but you're no stranger to a fish supper, hen".

I always hated first dates they were hard work trying to think of something to say, and overthinking it made you just talk a load of shit, and the bird would run a mile. One time I went on a date and I met the girl's mum and dad before we went for dinner.

So, sitting at the meal I'm thinking of shit to say and I hit out with, ","your parents seem nice,"

and she says, "yes, they are, thanks,"

and I come back with, "you're the double of your dad

and she spits out her drink all over me and says, while laughing, "I'm adopted!"

Beam me up Scotty...

So what now for me without sounding like Mark Renton from 'Trainspotting' saying I have the big TV washing machine, all that shit. I don't know what's next. I think when you hit forty you have two choices - grow old like Mick Jagger or Keith Richards: the first being the most sensible choice,

I mean, it's OK to be like Keith - that's fun, but remember he's a millionaire so he can afford to pay someone to wipe his ass when old age and the drink catches up with him. No, you just have to surrender to the fact that you're getting on in life. You drink light beer and the only pills you pop now are esomeprazole and vitamin D, and you check your watch to see how many steps you've done today so you can pat yourself on the back. And just when you think life couldn't get any more shit, covid-19 hits the streets and at first everyone thinks it's funny because it's only in China - you remember when all them cunts on Facebook were posting photos of themselves with bottles of Corona beer saying, 'won't make work tomorrow, I have the Corona virus lol'. Wankers! They were the same fuckers who were panic buying, then going on Facebook to tell people to stop panic buying while they were waiting for their Tesco online shop to show up for the third time that week. Panic buying was like doing heroin. No one admits to doing it, but some cunt is. Now after months of lockdown we are all free to go shopping, free to go to the movies, free to go for a meal, free to go on holiday. Me, I just want a pint in the Argosy. I know I never change but for some guys the pub shutting - it's like the love of your life turning into a cow. It's heart-breaking. It's their life and now the news says the pubs won't be allowed too many people in at a time, and they will take your details, and you will have to wear a mask and get in line. Imagine having a wee hangover, choking for a cold pint of beer, standing in a line outside the pub for 20 minutes with your mask on, only to realise at the end of the line you were in the queue for the fucking Kwik Fit next door to the pub. And how weird is it putting a mask on before you go into the pub. Most of my pals got the jail for doing that years ago. Taking your details is a good one and I'm glad I'm no' a young guy nowadays. I mean think back to all the pubs you were in over the years and all the times it kicked off. Imagine if they had your details. Fucking hell! I would be doing life.

See that's me, away again ranting like an old man. You can't escape it even if you tell yourself 'I won't do that when I'm older' it happens. I remember I was about 17, sitting with my dad and his old work pal, Tony. Now Tony was deaf and he didn't say too much, but that day a woman walked in with a wee girl who was about 4 years old. The woman tells the wee girl to stand at the door so mum can go talk to grandad.

As the wee girl is standing at the door Tony says to me, "look at that wee girl, ain't she sweet?"

and I go, "yeah, they're so cute at that age,"

and Tony says, "I bet in 20 years she'll make some poor guy's life a fucking living hell".

I always listened to the guys in the pub. I mean, they had been there and done it so they must know the score. Big Gerry told me the best way to get someone out of your life was to lend them money; sometimes it's money well spent. Nowadays you just block them on Facebook, job done. Don't need to see that cunt on my phone anymore. Another wee rant is people going for a beer and sitting on their phones. What's that all about? Before you leave the house tell your kids they are on that PS4 too much or that "your iPad is never out of your hands," then go for a pint and don't even know if it was a good pint because you were too busy looking at birds on Instagram; then maybe get another pint while you delete your search history before you go home to the wife.

She'll asks "how's the new phone,"

and you'll say, "it's OK, still trying to get the hang of it, Honey, but the beer was good, I think".

While I was just wanting a pint the whole country was wanting a holiday. They were craving two weeks in the sun, sitting by a mobbed pool, drinking cheap beer and munching a big bag of Lay's crisps. Sounds good really. My kids think that's a holiday and that's my fault because we went to Spain and wherever every year, but when I was a kid….hold on - old man rant again. Yeah, when I was a kid we went to Blackpool if we had the money. If my mum was struggling we went to my Aunt Jean's in Arbroath, and Arbroath was a much better holiday. Me and my two brothers grew up in a council flat so getting a train to Arbroath to my aunt's three bedroom up and down stairs, back and front door, was the best holiday ever. She had a dog we could pet to death. I mean, we didn't leave it alone. After about a day the dog was looking at us like, fuck off back to Pollok. When you went out the back, if you jumped over the fence on one side you were in a swing park, if you jumped over the other side you were in a farm. So for about a week me and my brothers would get along with each other and he'd push me on the swings, or we'd go over to the farm and push the cows over and steal the milk from the door steps early in the morning. We would think this is amazing - free milk. One day we went strawberry picking. The farmer gave you a bucket and you filled it with strawberries - easy - and when it was full he weighed it and you got paid. We were standing in the queue when a guy in front of us took a piss in his to make it even heavier for more money. My brothers were wanting to do it but none of us were needing a piss. As the guy got his weighed the farmer took a handful and told the guy to eat them and the fucker did it. Now that's a holiday! Fuck going to Blackpool; it's shit. People say Blackpool is our Las Vegas. Is that right? The only cunts that say that are cunts from Blackpool.

With everyone wanting away because of lockdown and the stress of it all more people are going up north seeing the highlands and all the lochs, putting money back into our own country. I mean, places like Spain are missing us more than we are missing them. And if you're feeling the stress of all this there is nothing makes you sleep better at night then being in the fresh air all day and that's the truth. When you're out in the middle of nowhere breathing it in, you will sleep like a baby. Sleep like a baby is a daft saying - I don't remember my kids sleeping much as a baby. Anyway stress, the worst thing about it is the lack of sleep; you know - when you're wanting your bed all day and then at bedtime you're brain wakes up to think mad shit at a hundred miles an hour: daft shit like, would you be killed in game of thrones if you had sciatica because you couldn't bend the knee. When I was going away to Spain and Greece as a young guy the boys in the pub looked at me like I was Indiana Jones. I would bring back tobacco and cigarettes and they would want to hear all my stories of being in a faraway land, because these guy only ever got as far as Blackpool, so they would love hearing about the golden sun, the blue sea, and most of all, how it was only 80p a pint and twenty fags for under a pound. Big Gerry did the tobacco run to France a few times and took a few of the guys with him because you were only allowed so much tobacco per person, so a few guys got a day away on a mini bus to a cash and carry in France and got paid in tobacco for going. Rab Fraser was the only other guy apart from me who went away to Spain, but he didn't fly, he went on his motorbike with his wife on the back. I always thought that sounds amazing and hard work at the same time but when he would tell you about his days of taking the back roads, finding a wee village and getting drunk for the night it sounded like a good time. The cheap holidays to Spain will come back and we will all go but before we do, see your own country first. I mean, some of the best places in the world are up the road for us Scots, so do what any one should do in a bad situation, find the good in it and go and sit at a loch, watch the sun set, drink beer or tea by the fire and don't forget your Skin so Soft .

This lockdown shit won't go away any time soon; we will be in and out of it for a while. Sure it's all about keeping everyone safe but it's a good way to run the country, too. The rich will always fuck the poor, that's just life, but now they can tell us what to do and say it's all because of this covid-19. I mean, this green list shit about what country you can go to; they say you can go to Australia or New Zealand and we are like, OK, thanks, just give me three years to save up a few grand so I can go. Thanks. These fuckers know the working class can't afford to go to Dubai, so then they go, well OK, just stay here and holiday in the UK and put all your hard earned cash back into this country, while all the rich fuck off to the sun. Sorry I'm ranting again - told you I'm getting old. When you are in your twenties and thirties you don't care about time, but in your forties and fifties time doesn't care about you... Steven Taylor from Aerosmith said life is like toilet paper, the closer you get to the end the faster it goes, and it's funny because it's true. When you're young and wild the summers last for ever, you don't get the fear and life is just a party, but then time comes sneaking up behind you and old age sets in day by day, and that's how you don't notice it. Ask your grandmother or grandfather - they will tell you, one minute they were young and busy bringing up the kids and then bang, old fuckers smelling of piss.

This is how I see getting old happens. They say if you put a frog in hot water it will scream for its life and try all it can to get out, but if you put a frog in cold water and slowly heat the water the poor wee frog will just accept it and sit in the water no matter how hot it gets till it's cooked, and that's why we don't see it, because if we got grey hair, a sore back and three day hangovers all at the one time we would go nuts, but we don't. We get all the shit over the years and don't notice it, or we don't want to accept that it's happening. You know, like when the kids come along so you stay in more and you think OK, I'll just have a wee drink at home, and that's fine. You put the kids to bed and bust a can open and after a few the wife goes to bed, but you stay up because you're a greedy fucker and you want a few Jack Daniel's, and more beer and before you know it you have the headphones on singing badly till about 4 in the morning.

When your wife gets up she finds you on the floor with an empty bottle of Jack and CDs all around you and she says, "you been up all night?"

and you're like, "yeah, I started listening to The Stones and forgot the time, you know how it is Honey," just as your kids are picking up the CD cases and asking, "who is Abba and Neil Diamond, daddy?"

And you're like, "never mind, put them away."

And then the next thing you would do was head for the pub for a hangover cure, it didn't matter the weather, you would always make it and as soon as you got to the pub door you could hear all the voices. It was like a warm blanket on a cold night. You would walk in, someone would have a beer waiting on you, it was like a bright star shining in the night. You would walk up to it like Indiana Jones about to grab it, but no wait you can't go out to the pub because you need to help out with the kids today, so what you do now while you have a cunt of a hangover is sit and feed one of your kids hot Weetabix, and watch some shit DVD like 'Barney and Friends'. You've only seen it about a million fucking times. Gone are the days of being in the pub that much you help the barmaid to the bank to get change and you get a free beer for it. I mean, free beer how good does that sound? Or sitting with the boys drinking all day and the only thing you had to worry about was making your work in the morning.

Day by day it goes away. You getting busy watching game shows and taking the family out for dinner. That's why they sell beer in places like Frankie and Benny's – it's to numb the pain. You know, like when you're out Christmas shopping with your wife and someone asks you "how's life" and you say, "taking forever". But don't worry you will get used to it and before you know it you'll be in TGI Fridays and it will be that busy and taking so long to get service that you will look at your watch and say its 8:30pm. fuck me, we're out late tonight gang.

Your life will change like the weather and you will think you won't be happy but you will. I mean, when a guy goes to jail, the day he gets his sentence when the judge says "twelve years, take him away" that guy is in a world of hurt but ten years later when he gets told he's out for good behaviour, that puts the wind up him too, because his brain can't take it all in. All he knows is the inside, it's all about accepting the change. And don't spend your life wishing you were rich; that won't do you any good, that's like wishing for the sun in Scotland - your life will be shit if you spend your time wishing it all away. And being rich isn't all that it's cracked up to be anyway. Being rich just gives you more ways to die. Think about it. If you're poor, will you ever fall off Mount Everest or crash land in your first class seat in Las Vegas? No, because when you're poor you can't afford shit, and the only reason I'm telling you this is because I was sitting in the pub one day and big Gerry Law worked out that I was the only guy in the pub who might one day die in a plane crash, because I was the only cunt in the Argosy who went on fucking holiday. And another thing about having money is it brings its own problems, and I know you're thinking I'm OK with that, but your other problems when you're poor don't go away, so you just go from problems like your wife giving you a hard time about spending too much money on beer to when you're rich she will just turn that round to drinking too much. Or then you will get the rich problems you would never get before, like your wife thinks the housemaid Is using her vibrator.

Isn't life just taking for ever? Sorry I'm on a rant again I know, but some things just get on my tits. Like when you watch a programme on TV and they are getting people to try a new wine or whisky. You know these wine tasters - fuck me. What a job! Paid to drink wine. I never saw that job in the dole office. I would always fall for the bullshit they talk. They would take a sip of some whisky and rave about it, saying they could taste the caramel or the vanilla, and I would be thinking that sounds like the whisky for me, that sounds so sweet - I need to get a bottle before it's sold out. And I would be a sucker and buy a bottle, take it home and pour a large glass because it's OK, it's going to be sweet and warm, and then bang - it's just another fucking same old whisky. Bastards! Every time I would fall for it. There would be no taste of sweet blackberry in my new wine - no it would be as bitter as vinegar. If you want sweet wine get Eldorado or Buckfast.

And one more thing before I finish this wee rant; another thing we should get is we should be treated better when we have a cold. I mean, think about it. You work hard, pay your bills and be a law abiding person, but when you get the cold and go to the doctor all he will say is "go home, have a Lemsip, drink lots of fluids and take it easy". Come on, take it easy? We can't take it fucking easy. We have to go to work or deal with the kids. I mean, when you get a right bad shitty cold, when your bones are sore and your head feels like some cunt is having a rave in it, the last thing that you need is paracetamol. No. I think if you pay your taxes and work hard the doctor should be allowed to give you a two week sick line and some sleeping pills so you can just go to bed and sleep through the cold. Now how good does that sound? Life's hard enough without getting the flu and still going to work, high on Lemsip and looking like the walking dead. In Scotland when you have a cold you're told to have a hot toddy which is hot whisky, honey and lemonade, and a lot better than a fucking Lemsip. My mum says when my old man would get the cold he would heat up a half bottle of Eldorado, but she thinks it was just an excuse to have more drink. Well the apple doesn't fall far from the tree, because the last time I had a cold I had a cappuccino and honey Jack Daniel's. How times change.

So in 2021 COP26 hit Glasgow; every world leader came to our city to talk about the planet getting too warm. Funny thing is everyone from Glasgow has spent their entire lives wishing it was a bit hotter. You will never hear a guy from Glasgow saying, "fuck me, it's too hot" or "I wish it would rain for just a few more days". But jokes aside, I'm all for looking after the planet, but these leaders tuning up in their privet jets and running from town to town in twenty cars for one guy makes no sense at all. COP26 is like having a women's rights meeting in a strip club; it's a joke, and on top of it all we have the young team blaming us for it all. They're out in town, stuck to some bridge with superglue shouting that we have destroyed their future. Fuck off. Tell me this. Who is it who gets takeaways three or four time a week? It's no' me. I get one, maybe on my night off. I'm no' at McDonald's stuffing my face or getting 2 pizzas on a Tuesday night. No, it's the superglue kids and their take away boxes, all the pizza boxes the size of a coffee table that you can't recycle because they are covered in grease, all going in the bin. But the kids have a bamboo toothbrush because plastic is bad. Now I know better than anyone how bad plastic is, but I don't blame my granny for it because it was about in the fifties and sixties, too. No, but these wee fuckers want to blame my generation.

That's an American thing to blame your parents. In America you can do whatever you like, and when you get caught you sit down with a psychiatrist and they will ask you, "why did you kill that guy," and you can say, "because my father didn't hug me as a child," or "why did you rape that girl" is "because my mum didn't breastfeed me". It's a way of saying, "yeah, I'm a cunt but it's no' my fault" so I'm saying the world heating up is no' my generation's fault. We didn't have fast food as kids, we didn't drink out of plastic bottles - it was glass and we returned them into use again, and we only got a takeaway once a month if we were lucky, and only went out for dinner once every five years. And in the summer we went on holiday to Blackpool or up north in Scotland. We didn't jet off to Ibiza for two weeks drinking from plastic cups and eating out of polystyrene boxes. No we were in Blackpool eating fish and chips out of an old newspaper, and our treat was a few sweets in a brown paper bag. We weren't out all night clubbing, high on drugs, popping pills and sucking laughing gas. And all the years I went to school I never once got dropped off in a car. No, I walked like the rest of my pals; now kids get a lift to school then go out at the weekends to TGI Fridays or the Odeon. Me and my pals in Pollok had fuck all like that. We sat about the streets playing hide and seek because we didn't have anywhere to go. We only had each other; we were all in the same boat.

Thinking back now, the days growing up in Pollok were so different to kids' lives now. We were stuck in the middle of nowhere but we didn't know any better. We most of us came from broken homes but no one ever complained about it. We just all stuck together and stayed out day and night. I mean, even in the middle of winter some of the mums couldn't get their kids to come in, it was always "five more minutes, ma". We didn't have internet or a TV in our room with a PS and Netflix. We were lucky to have our own room back then, so that's why we stayed out as late as we could, because going home meant tea and toast then to bed. But I remember me and all the boys and the girls were happy. Like I said Pollok was in the middle of nowhere so we didn't know there was a better life out there. We were happy in our own Westworld; when you have nothing you have nothing to lose, as they say. The sad thing about being kids today is they watch all the shit on TV, like keeping up with the you know who, and they sit in their wee nice houses, but think it's shit because they want what the people on TV have, the big mansion and the sunshine. Wishing you were someone else is the saddest thing ever and too many kids today are doing it. They should be out playing two man hunt or stealing apples off the farm, and on a Friday drink a few snake bites up in the field. Nothing better than sitting on a burnt out car, drinking a beer on a summer's night knowing you have seven weeks off school.

If I was to end this book with one word that says it all

you would think it would be love, or some bullshit like that, and sure these words like love and family mean a lot to me. But I grew up in Glasgow and if you go about shouting about love everyone will laugh in your face right after they've beaten you up. So one word that will keep you going in a hard city like Glasgow is... pals.. Billy the Kid's favourite word. He said if you have one or two good pals, then you can take on an army. You might no' win but it is always good to have back up. Having pals keeps you young. We all hate growing older, it's well...growing up...I don't like. All that 'act you're age' bullshit. Don't fall for that. Anyone who tells you to act your age, get them a one way ticket out of your life fast, because you can act daft and still be a good dad; it will keep you young and happy. And don't worry about getting old; it's coming whether you like it or not. As sure as rain will fall from a Scottish sky you will hit 30 then 40 and so on. and one day you will get up and think how the fuck did I get here - a 40 year old guy with wife and kids and a mortgage so big the fucking Hubble telescope can't see the end of it. It's all part of the master plan. You will see the signs of getting old, like:

1. Taxi drivers are younger than you, like when you get into a taxi and this wee boy says "alright mate, where you off too?" And you're like, "does your dad know you stole his car, wee man".

2. Remember when you were young stuck in the house watching TV and had no money, bored out of your mind? Well now you call that relaxing.

3. As a young guy you would go out drinking and taking drugs for three or four days straight and still make your work?

Well now you have three cans of beer watching 'Who Wants to be a Millionaire' on TV and you wake up feeling like you've been in Ibiza for three weeks, and now the only drug you take is paracetamol to get over your three beers.

4. Drinks change names and go up in price, like Diamond Whites were good and cheap, then they take the sugar out of them and stick a fucking cork in it and call it Pasco.

I always try not to rant like some old tit but you can't fight it. I suffer with TMB (too many birthdays).. sure life is no' the same and I miss my pals that are now behind the sun, and all my heroes are gone or worse - they have gotten old. I mean, Keith Richards is off the drink! Never did I think I would see that happening. Rod Stewart sings more about Grace than Maggie May or Baby Jane, and don't start me on Bono - that fucker talks more on stage than he fucking sings. And my hero, Billy Connolly, he went on Parkinson that much he caught it off him. If you were to ask me do I miss the old days sitting in the pub drinking and smoking, I would tell you yes. I miss it very much, but it's my pals and maybe my youth I miss, not the drink or the drugs. And I'm glad I did it when I was young and could recover from it. Would I do it all again ? No, not just now. Maybe when my kids get older and don't need me and I'm this 70 year old guy I would love to go back to drinking and smoking and maybe get too old to die young, tattoo done. But for now I'm a happy man with a wife who is my best pal, and two kids, Shawnay and Lucas, who keep me busy and make me laugh every day. So why would I miss all that just to sit in a pub? I know I go on a bit about all my pals being gone but as much as God, or whoever it is pushing the buttons up there, has taken my pals away, well, they have given me a family a new gang. I was talking to my daughter, Shawnay, one day and she said something cheeky to me so I did the father thing and said, "I would have never have spoken to my dad like that at your age," and she hit back with "well I know that because you didn't know your dad at my age"... Kids, you got to love them because no cunt else will. When my dad passed away I got his Elvis records. When I go my kids get a fucking house...

Printed in Great Britain
by Amazon